The Style Hongrois *in the Music of Western Europe*

Music advisor to Northeastern University Press
GUNTHER SCHULLER

THE *Style Hongrois*
IN THE MUSIC OF
WESTERN EUROPE

JONATHAN BELLMAN

Northeastern University Press
BOSTON

Northeastern University Press

Copyright 1993 by Jonathan Bellman

Library of Congress Cataloging-in-Publication Data

Bellman, Jonathan, 1957–
    The style hongrois in the music of Western Europe /
Jonathan Bellman.
        p.   cm.
        Includes bibliographical references and index.
        ISBN 1-55553-169-5 (cloth: acid-free paper)
        1. Music—Europe—18th century—Hungarian
influences. 2. Music—
Europe—19th century—Hungarian influences.   I. Title.
    ML240.B37   1993   93-10150
    780'.9'033—dc20

Designed by Ann Twombly

Composed in Bembo by Coghill Composition Company in
Richmond, Virginia. Printed and bound by The Maple Press
Company in York, Pennsylvania. The paper is Sebago
Antique, an acid-free sheet.

MANUFACTURED IN THE UNITED STATES OF AMERICA
97 96 95 94 93   5 4 3 2 1

Contents

Acknowledgments

IT IS ONE of the privileges of authorship that one may express gratitude to friends, colleagues, and all those who have offered support and help in the course of the work in question. This is one of the most enjoyable aspects of writing a book. Although I really owe a debt of thanks to many more than are listed here, I can only, in this space, try to remember the foremost among them.

First, let me thank the National Endowment for the Humanities, which awarded me a Summer Stipend in 1992; the bulk of the writing took place during that time. William A. Frohlich and Gunther Schuller of Northeastern University Press took an early interest in my work and were both helpful and encouraging in the various stages of the book's development.

It was my pleasure to study with Leonard Ratner when I was a graduate student at Stanford University; his approach to musical conventions and their extramusical associations has had great significance for me and this book. Tom Grey, in reading the manuscript and making suggestions, strengthened its presentation immeasurably. George Barth, who has long served as a model in the areas of both scholarship and performance, has been a sounding board and critic for many of my ideas. I have often benefited from his laser-accurate advice and criticism.

Hansmartin and Christine Zeuner were of tremendous assistance in locating and copying hard-to-find sources in German libraries. Steve Whiting offered some very beneficial advice on locating historical Gypsy sources, and Ian Hancock of the International Romani Union offered both encouragement and great help with Romani sources in general. My friend and former student Paula Durbin produced the index with expedition and good humor. For encouragement when things became particularly frustrating, my friends Shelley Davis and John Nathan Gootherts are particularly deserving of thanks. My parents and family have likewise been of great help and support.

My wife, Deborah Kauffman, provided all the musical examples and many of the German translations, a substantial amount of work. More importantly, she provided constant encouragement, help, and a thousand different aids in making the writing of this book a less exhausting process. It is to her, and to our three-month-old son, Benjamin Howard Bellman, that this book is lovingly dedicated.

STANFORD, CALIFORNIA
FEBRUARY, 1993

The Style Hongrois *in the Music of Western Europe*

Introduction

A STUDY such as this must of necessity draw on a wide range of resources, and it may therefore be helpful to outline a few of the most important. Central, of course, are the musical scores themselves. The Turkish Style thrived from roughly Gluck's time through Beethoven's; the *style hongrois* appeared in Haydn's time and continued to be used until Ravel's and even beyond. The task of distilling "Turkish" and "Gypsy" languages from the works that feature them is, procedurally at least, relatively uncomplicated because each body of relevant musical gestures was finite, and the same ones were used throughout Europe. In the *style hongrois,* each of these familiar figures, textures, or usages is traceable to some aspect of either Hungarian music or the Gypsies' manner of performing it. Rediscovering the historical circumstances and the cultural environment in which this language was heard and understood is, of course, much less straightforward.

To this point, the Turkish Style has excited far more interest and commentary than has the *style hongrois.* One excellent treatment of it appears in Miriam Karpilow Whaples's doctoral dissertation, *Exoticism in Dramatic Music, 1600–1800*.[1] In addition to identifying the style's musical features, she provides an overview of the "Turkish" operas in which they were used and examines the first-person accounts of those who actually heard the Turkish musicians play the supposed source music that composers would later try to evoke. My own overview is also much indebted to Thomas Bauman's discussion of the Turkish Style in his book on Mozart's *Abduction from the Seraglio*;[2] he not only outlines the component gestures of the style, but also discusses the popular image of the Turk to which such musical references applied. Thus, not only what was said musically is illuminated but also, in a sense, what it meant.

Discussions of the *style hongrois* in the scholarly literature tend to be general and, even at that, few and far between. Contemporary perceptions of the Gypsies as a people may be found in works of literature, where characterizations are dramatic and plentiful. These must be treated with care; they were widely read and were instrumental in forming the Gypsies' popular reputation, but as fiction and poetry they cannot even pretend to verity. Far more compelling are the contemporary "nonfiction" accounts, which began to appear in the late seventeenth century and are found mainly in two types of sources: encyclopedias and travelogues written by foreigners visiting Hungary. Accounts of this kind reflect some factual material, the authors' own observations and personal biases, and (like the fictional accounts) a good amount of popular stereotype. All of these factors are necessary to an understanding of the impression the *style hongrois* made on the listeners of the time.

One scholarly study requires specific mention. Bálint Sárosi's *Gypsy Music* is an exhaustive treatment of the sources relating to the Hungarian Gypsies themselves and their musical activities, starting with their first appearance in that country.[3] Sárosi also examines the *verbunkos* and other music that the Gypsies were known to play. For my study, it is an indispensable resource; as my primary concern is how the Gypsies' music was received, understood, and imitated by non-Gypsies and non-Hungarians in western Europe, a thorough study of its actual roots is invaluable. Sárosi provides this, as well as the historical and musical background of the Hungarian and Gypsy reality from which the *style hongrois* evolved.

Surprisingly, the first major discussion of this musical language had to wait for Liszt's highly problematic book, written some time after the style had evolved and matured. In a way, the pattern is similar to the reception of jazz in the twentieth century. Jazz was popular, initially had dubious demimonde associations, was either passionately embraced or reviled, but was not the subject of much serious discussion (as opposed to partisan squabbling) until well after its presence and popularity were established. Most importantly for the historian, with jazz we at least have sound documents (that is, early recordings) to guide our understanding of the way the musical language emerged and evolved and why people responded to it the way they did.

In the case of the *style hongrois*, the first recordings of actual Hungarian-Gypsy bands date from more than two centuries after the first ones emerged from Hungary and are therefore of limited use in documenting the style's development. Today, echoes of their performance style occasionally are heard in the performances of musicians from Hungary, or of those who may have studied with someone conversant with the style, but any kind of global understanding is almost unheard-of. In the absence of recordings, verbal descriptions of those who heard this music can illuminate, to a limited extent, what it must have been like. Aside from that, all we have is a broad stratum of secondary source material: Western art music, and the far less inspired body of *Hausmusik* imitating it, utilizing the *style hongrois*. This repertoire has a long history, an unmistakable sound, and a unique historical context. The best works of this kind, moreover, maintain a persistent popularity. It was in the collection of this musical and extramusical record that this study took shape.

Let me add a word or two about terminology. As will be explained in due course, controversies have raged over whether this was actually Gypsy music or Hungarian music. *Style hongrois* has long meant music evocative of the Hungarian-Gypsy context, and so I use this phrase as much as possible. However, I also consider it appropriate to use *Hungarian* in specific reference to the musical content, almost all of which is independently Hungarian, and also to use *Gypsy* for the performance characteristics and to link it with those who both performed it in Hungary and disseminated it as they moved westward. I certainly hope to avoid further confusion of what in the nineteenth century became a highly politicized issue, but it also must be acknowledged that the accurate use of both terms involves a great overlap. Since the music was the product of both cultures, it can be the exclusive property of neither.

Some inconsistency in orthography (American *Gypsy* vs. British *Gipsy*) is unavoidable. I favor the American spelling but try to leave the British intact when it is in the context of a quote or citation. Similarly, because *Ingharese, Ongherese,* and *Ungherese,* among the variants, were all used by individual composers, I allow their spellings to remain as they chose them. I follow the same pattern of nonintervention with archaic spellings.

In many historical sources qualities and characteristics are imputed to the Gypsies that reflect far more about European bigotries, fears, and desires than about reality. The Gypsies in my study are popular-culture Gypsies, those the Europeans only assumed they knew and understood. Studies of the real circumstances of the Romani people throughout history and in the present day belong to a different field altogether, the center and clearinghouse for which is the International Romani Union (Manchaca, Texas 78652-0822). The views associated with the Gypsies and the *style hongrois* documented in this study should not be consulted for any kind of authority regarding the true nature of the Romani people.

PART ONE

CHAPTER I

Provenance and Musical Origins

I

THE *style hongrois* (literally, "Hungarian style") refers to the specific musical language used by Western composers from the mid-eighteenth to the twentieth centuries to evoke the performances of Hungarian Gypsies. The use of the French appellation rather than an English one is a bow to tradition; *style hongrois* has long meant the Hungarian-Gypsy writing of Haydn, Schubert, Liszt, and others, whereas the English phrase "Hungarian style" might be taken to mean real Hungarian folk music of the sort that interested Bartók and Kodály. Because they emerged from Hungary, Hungarian Gypsies have incorrectly been called "Hungarians" in some of the countries in which they later found themselves;[1] moreover, since the musical materials of this style are almost exclusively Hungarian in origin, the term *Hungarian* has been associated with the style more than the term *Gypsy*.

The distinction is important because of the primary components of the style. The source music on which Schubert,

Liszt, Brahms, and others would draw was not a purely Hungarian music, but a combination of Hungarian popular song and dance repertories with the performance style and interpretive traditions of the Gypsies, who were the most prominent musicians in Hungary and who disseminated Hungarian music as they left and moved westward. In its earliest form, the *style hongrois* began to appear in Viennese Classical music as a small body of inflections that might lend a piano trio or string quartet movement the character of an *ongherese*. What this meant, in German terms, was slightly exotic or "characteristic" but no more disruptively so than the highly popular Turkish Style, with which the *style hongrois* overlapped somewhat in terms of both chronology and specific content. A century later it had blossomed into a discrete musical vernacular, suitable for supporting such discourses as the concentrated Gypsy essays of the Romantics. It is also during this time that the multifaceted stereotype of the Gypsies as a people was taking root in the popular culture, and as a result the *style hongrois* began to accrue meanings and assume a significance inaccessible to the more common musical styles. As the dialect flowered, composers could use it to express the previously inexpressible.

The *style hongrois* represents the first wholesale and conscious embrace of a popular music associated with a lower societal caste by the composers and listeners of more formal, schooled music. This would happen again with the emergence of certain folk musics in the service of nationalism in the nineteenth century and jazz in the twentieth. The process was the same in the eighteenth and nineteenth centuries as it would be later: composers of art music first had to "discover" a vernacular music that had already been in existence for a substantial length of time and then, gradually, appropriate it for their own purposes.

What these purposes were would be defined by its unique

character and capabilities. The study of any language is by nature twofold, and only the more superficial stage defines its constituent parts, the words and grammar. On a deeper level, such a study examines those ideas or emotions the language is (perhaps uniquely) suitable to express, thereby defining what and how it communicates *differently* from other languages. In other words, it describes both what the language is and what it is not. Therefore, the study of a specific musical language such as the *style hongrois* has both to examine the musical speech itself and to illuminate the need for it, that is, to identify those things the conventional musical language of the time was unable to express.

That the dialect was understood to be a separate entity is proven by the fact that the gestures of which it is composed appear in the works of a wide variety of composers, and that its appearance always has the same extraordinary, exotic sound. With isolated exceptions, though, it was rarely discussed in print, at least until Liszt's book *Des Bohémiens et de leur musique en Hongrie* came out in 1859. Musicians' travelogues do not mention it at all, and (more surprisingly) neither do recent musical studies of Vienna by Gartenberg, Hanson, Hilmar, and Osborne.[2] This silence illustrates its nature as a popular musical vernacular: the musical record of its presence indicates that it must have been very commonly heard and well understood, but seemingly so much so that no one bothered with descriptions or explanations that later musicians could investigate.

As an example of the reverse journey from vernacular language to concert language, the *style hongrois* represents something of a turning point in the history of music. Its immediate predecessor as a standardized exotic musical dialect, the Turkish Style (or Janissary style, or *stilo alla turca*), evolved from a sort of battle music played by Turkish military bands outside the walls of Vienna during the siege of that city in 1683. Relatively few had heard the Turks play in the first place, and virtually no one remembered it with any degree of accuracy, so no one had much of an idea what it sounded like. As we will see in chapter 2, what became understood as the Turkish Style was thus almost entirely the product of the European imagination.

The *style hongrois*, by contrast, derived from the exotic-sounding music played by Gypsy bands (not actual Magyars) in Hungary and westward to Vienna. As time passed, composers imitated and idealized the music they had heard, interpreting it as a Hungarian national style. To a limited extent, then, early manifestations of the *style hongrois* (at that time often called *ongherese*) may have been regarded in a way similar to more standard but highly conventionalized foreign styles: French overtures, Italian opera sinfonias, or stylized foreign dance types such as the polonaise or bolero. It differed from the Turkish Style in that the earlier style had not been heard by the musicians "imitating" it and so was largely synthesized, but Hungarian Gypsies could easily be heard in person. What was incomplete was both awareness of the music's origins and any real understanding of the people performing it.

In comparing the two styles, it should be remembered that there are points of historical and musical connection between the Gypsies and the Turks. The Gypsies emerged from the east, and as we shall see later, were for that reason often suspected, in threatening times, of having Turkish sympathies. Neither group was trusted; both were objects of satire. Some Gypsy musical traditions survived from lands further east: for example, Sárosi points out that in Turkey and Greece as well as in other lands, the typical Gypsy musical ensemble is a duo, consisting of a drum and a kind of oboe called a *zurna* or *zurla*. The same combination survived in Hungary proper at least until the eighteenth century, although the instruments themselves had primarily military associations. When they were played in military contexts it was by Hungarian peasants, not Gypsies.[3] This eastern oboe had enjoyed sufficient popularity to acquire a Hungarian name, the *tárogató*, and probably predated the Gypsies' arrival there. Moreover, the association of "Gypsy" with "musician" was by the eighteenth century already a long tradition.

The Gypsies call themselves *Rom*. The *American Heritage Dictionary* defines the adjective *Romany* (an old spelling; the more modern *Romani* is preferred) as "of or pertaining to the Gypsies, their culture, or their language." The etymology for this word is given as "Romany *Romani*, plural of *romano*, gypsy, from *rom*, man, husband, gypsy man, from Sanskrit *domba, doma*, man of a low caste of musicians."[4] The association of Gypsies with music is thus an ancient one; indeed, as Sárosi points out, in Hungary, Turkey, and Greece the words for *Gypsy* mean the musical occupation, regardless of whether or not the musician in question is an actual Gypsy.[5] This natural disposition to music, remarked upon by the Gypsies' most virulent foes as well as their greatest admirers, was a particular benefit in Hungary, where societal constraints effectively prevented Hungarians from entering the sphere of professional music.

Indeed, the Gypsies came to be understood as essentially the Hungarian musical caste. Rev. Robert Walsh, travelling in 1828, describes them as such after hearing a pair of wind players at an inn: "They played duets in good time and tune; and, in fact, are the musicians of Hungary."[6] Writing somewhat later (1844), Johann Georg Kohl felt that all "Hungarian" musicians were either German or Gypsy: the Germans had the leading positions and the Gypsies played under them.[7] And it was Liszt's crediting the Gypsies with the outright creation of what was a fundamentally Hungarian music that led to a real journalistic firestorm fifteen to twenty years after that.

De facto Romani hegemony in Hungarian music was only partially the result of any natural musical ability Gypsies may have possessed; they were also helped by social circumstances. Hungary since the Counter-Reformation had nurtured strong social conventions proscribing violin playing, other music making, and (practically speaking) entertainment of any kind. The threat posed by the Reformation left the Catholic Church even more negatively inclined toward music and dancing than the medievals had been, and the Gypsies were ready and able to fill the void.[8] An increase in talented Gypsy musicians, passing the craft along from father to son, at the same time that indigenous Magyars were strongly discouraged from musical aspirations, eventually amounted to something approaching a race-specific musical occupation in Hungary, which eventually spawned this essentially race-specific musical dialect.

II

The music the Gypsies played originated in Hungary, but was not of pure folk derivation, and from this came a rather large misunderstanding. The debate of Gypsy versus Hungarian origin for this music would be maintained well into the twentieth century, with the awestruck Franz Liszt appearing on one side of the issue to claim exclusive Gypsy origin and enraged Hungarian nationals on the other. The Gypsies' practice of performing Hungarian music almost exclusively (as opposed to actual Romani songs) was well understood by this time. Gabor Matráy, a nineteenth-century Hungarian music librarian and scholar, wrote, "In our country we do not know of any music which bears the character of the Gypsy people,"[9] and this was essentially the point of view that would later be vindicated by the research of, among others, Béla Bartók.[10] There are various kinds of Romani folk music, and songs in the Romani language, but they have never been a part of the *style hongrois*. Gypsy musicians, having little interest in either self-documentation or academic debate, have remained largely without comment on the issue, preferring simply to play whatever music people want to hear. As is appropriate to a "musical caste," their motivation has always been practical.

This music was performed in two general styles, slow and fast. The slow variety is called *hallgató*, which in Hungarian means "to be listened to" (as opposed to being danced to). It is free and rhapsodic and, although its basis was a song literature, became wholly improvisatory, often in direct contradiction to the spirit of the lyrics. The other type of music is fast (*cifra* in Hungarian, meaning "flashy") and is intended for dancing. In many cases such music also began with a vocal model, which generations of improvisers had ornamented and embroidered, but the end result is a version of a very different character. It is this music that features prominently in the popular imagination as inspiring wild, frenzied dances with much heel clicking (although this certainly happens in slow dancing also). Naturally, the Gypsy musicians playing it were assumed to be abandoning themselves wholly to the music and the ancient griefs and passions of which it sang, and so compelling was the effect that to an Austrian or German, the music obviously bespoke the tribulation-filled history of the Gypsies. To a Hungarian-born listener, however, it was the distant Hungarian past that was being evoked.

The dance music with which the Gypsy musicians were most closely associated was originally called simply a *Magyar*, or Hungarian dance, and would only later become known as *verbunkos*. This term, a Hungarian word derived from the German *Werbung*, "recruitment," refers to music played by the Gypsies (often under duress) for the purpose of luring village boys into the army with depictions of a jolly, carefree army life. The dance seems to have produced a great dramatic effect, beginning slowly with measured, dignified steps from the commanding officer and becoming wilder and more joyous as men from further down the military hierarchy began to join in. General characteristics of *verbunkos* include duple meter, the gradual increase in tempo from very slow to very fast, and a great deal of instrumental ornamentation. The best discussion of *verbunkos* music is Sárosi's, which includes contemporary descriptions, cultural background, and musical analyses and examples.[11]

The cultural significance of this or any Hungarian dance music is far greater than its original context as a recruitment technique might suggest. Dancing as ritual, as a form of expression, and as a crucial aspect of living seems always to have been an extremely strong element in Magyar culture. In his short account of Hungarian music, Julius Kaldy noted such an instance:

> Our ancestors used to inter their dead with song and music. Priests of lower rank delivered an address at the funeral, praised the heroism and virtues of the dead, and at the end paced round the grave in a slow dance. This custom likewise remained partially until the present day. For at burials—with Catholic and Protestant alike—the Cantor takes leave of the dead in a mournful song. After the interment the mourners assemble with the sorrowing family at the funeral banquet. 160 years ago the "Dance of Death" used to be danced after this evening meal.
>
> This was probably the oldest Hungarian dance, which our people here danced for hundreds of years as a remnant of heathen funeral rites.[12]

Dance as a manifestation of Hungarian culture has always received special notice from foreigners introduced to it for the first time. The English traveller and mining engineer Edward Brown, visiting in the early 1670s, was struck by the

Magyars' manner of dancing, and his description shows that he sensed its ancient lineage:

> Before I came into *Hungary,* I observed no shadow or shew of the old *Pyrrhrical Saltation,* or warlike way of Dancing, which the Heyducks practice in this Country. They dance wth naked Swords in their hands, advancing, brandishing, and clashing the same, turning, winding, elevating, and depressing their bodies with strong and active motions; singing withal unto their measures, after the manner of the Greeks. [13]

The dances themselves reflected much about the Hungarian personality. Their history was tribal, equestrian, and nomadic, and the primary emotions associated with them were seriousness, courage, and freedom. A German officer wrote in 1792:

> [The Hungarian National Dance] expresses the character of the nation in an extraordinary way. Even the long trousers of the Hungarian point to a people whose living element is riding. . . . As a necessity in this the dancer must be spurred. The clicking of the spurs is indeed an essential part of the Hungarian dance. . . .
>
> The true Hungarian dances have to begin really slowly and then they must be continued faster. They are much more becoming to a serious moustached face than to a young lad no matter what forced capers they do. Even when the Hungarian dance does become somewhat livelier it is not so much a sanguine as a choleric liveliness which captures the dancer and in which he does not abandon the seriousness with which he was born; indeed it rather seems that he just gives more fiery and more courageous expression to the already mentioned freedom and independence of the dance. [14]

The fact is, much of the power and character of the expression of the Hungarian dance is a result of the individual element, prominent in this last passage. This aspect can even go as far as soloistic improvisation. A particularly picturesque description was written by the poet and philosopher A. de Gerando in 1845:

> The Hungarian dance adapts to happy and sorrowful melodies alike. It gives the dancer the opportunity to be free master over his steps and movements, these not being bound to any kind of rule. The dancer's sole business is to give off his own fire and to invent dance figures.[15]

These descriptions illustrate the deep cultural resonance of the dances that the Gypsies' music accompanied and help to explain the proprietary nationalistic vigor with which some have asserted and defended the essentially Hungarian nature of the music. It also casts some light on the peculiar importance and power attributed to Gypsy performances. The magic associated with Gypsy musicians stemmed from their personality and performance style, but was greatly enhanced by the fact that they were playing a music that itself struck a nationalistic chord in the souls of the original Hungarian listeners. It evoked their national identity, an identity all the more precious because of their history and frequent circumstance as a ruled people (a circumstance not unknown, of course, to the Gypsies). This character of the *verbunkos,* both music and dance, was something unique to Hungary, and thus a powerful music for the Gypsies to cultivate in their later performances.

Verbunkos was not the only source music at the Gypsies' disposal, however. They also drew on an active vocal repertorie, the *nóta* (literally, "melody,") songs, a genre Bartók called the "new style of peasant music." These songs were composed largely by minor nobles, people for whom professional musical performance and involvement would have been unthinkable, and were often sentimental in nature. They represented a Hungarian response to the German *Volksthüm-lieder,* a genre described by one scholar as "hackneyed tunes with slobbery texts,"[16] that were closely associated with *Singspiele.* The Hungarian derivative quickly gained popularity in the eighteenth century and was fast eclipsing the old Hungarian folk music later to be collected by Bartók and Kodály.

In the radical transformation from vocal to instrumental works, certain aspects of the songs' inherent character were still retained. The Hungaran texts of these pieces lent them a unique declamational character; these rhythms and articulations were then associated with the Gypsies who played them and finally were imitated by non-Hungarian-speaking composers in the absence of any text at all. Even when highly fragmented and ornamented, much of the unique character of the *nóta* songs stemmed from their angular, abrupt, and oddly punctuated melodic lines, which lent a kind of caprice to their slower pace and frequently sad or wistful mood.

The *czardas* is a traditional Hungarian national dance that survives to this day and may simply be a later form of *verbunkos.* It has two primary sections: *lassu* or *lassan* (slow) and *friss* or *friska* (from the German *frisch,* fresh or fast). The slow section is in a heavy, deliberate 4/4 meter and is more a presentation step than a dance. The fast section can be either one or several different dancing songs, which in their abandon hint at a total loss of emotional control. In the present day, a *czardas* performance can be simply a series of tunes ranging from very slow to fast. It is with this dance, or series of characteristic song and dance types, that the Gypsy musicians, as representatives of Hungary's westward-migrating musical caste, are most closely associated in the popular mind.

III

This rather general description of the Gypsies and the source repertories of the *style hongrois* will suffice in terms of what is relevant to this study. As the popularity of this style did not result from a profound nineteenth-century understanding of the music's origins, a thorough source investigation would be quite beside the point. Put simply, western musicians and audiences were smitten by a new and highly characteristic music, and they began to imitate it. What fueled its popularity and further defined its significance in contemporary culture was what it was *imagined* to be, not necessarily what it was, and what the Gypsies were *presumed* to be, not what they were. Since the Gypsies were outsiders, European society's fears and desires could easily be pinned on them, and it was only natural that the Gypsies' music in turn came to suggest these fears and desires to the European mind. When mainstream composers began to write more formal music using the *style hongrois,* one predictable effect it had on listeners was to evoke the same associations the original Gypsy performances did.

The origins of the Gypsies' characteristic performance accent might also be more straightforward than the heat of the later debate might suggest. Sárosi describes the increasing Gypsy presence in Hungarian music as follows:

> In the seventeenth century data on gypsy musicians disappear rather than increase. And yet at that time the number of gypsy musicians increased strikingly. It was just that they *no longer* caused any stir with their individual strange music-making, and they could *not yet* draw any attention to themselves with the role they had in Hungarian music.[17]

It is interesting that the music making of the Gypsies, later to command so much attention, does not seem to have excited much comment at this early time; this suggests they were making music in much the same way other Hungarians were. Sárosi himself suggests that a 1683 reference to "Hungarian fiddlers" probably includes Gypsies as well,[18] which in turn implies that at this point there was little to distinguish the Gypsies' music from that of the natives.

Hungarian music itself would not remain a stable entity, and was entering a period of profound change. In the eighteenth century, western styles dominated such upper-class environments as the Esterházy court, but an indigenous Hungarian music was still enjoyed by society at large. On the cultural front, this homegrown product was challenged by a "Germanophile" school that felt western musical schooling and traditions represented a higher and more cultivated level of musical development. The scholar Ferenc Verseghy (1757–1822) was at the center of a reform movement that sought to do away with such Hungarian archaisms as pentatonicism, ecclesiastical modes, and homophony. He castigated "the tunes wanting in rhythm and measure . . . the religious or secular sing-song of our country folk and those symphonies or rather dysphonias, aped as a rule by our Gypsies in such a miserable manner . . . which are the Gypsy tunes for dancing . . . to nothing better than the gait of someone tipsy who almost totters, without any order or regularity, sometimes with small steps, sometimes with larger steps."[19] Notice what is being censured: both the old, declamatory, and irregular Hungarian folk music of the sort that would be studied in the twentieth century, and the Gypsy performance of *verbunkos*. The Gypsies "ape" inferior (that is, Hungarian rather than German) music; they are not criticized for playing their own. Moreover, the instruments for which they became famous, such as the bagpipe and the aforementioned fiddle and *tárogató,* were instruments well known in Hungary and originally characteristic of Hungarian music making.

Those criticizing the Gypsies' performance style for lack of skill, excessive ornamentation, or for their heterophonic performances of dance tunes (which followed older Hungarian practice, not the German approach that featured bass and counterpoint), were those whose sympathies compelled them to look westward for the "improvement" of Hungarian music.[20] As the Gypsies remained socially a group apart, it seems likely that they simply continued in the old traditions. Gestures and features that were quickly becoming distant, archaic, and ultimately foreign-sounding in the changing musical environment came to be associated with the Gypsy performance vocabulary. In maintaining this disappearing Hungarian musical language, their performances took on the power of the sort of folk music that touches the deepest regions of national consciousness and became highly suggestive to all of Europe, not the Hungarians alone.

Before we proceed to the dialect that evolved from the Gypsies' performances, though, its main forerunner as an "exotic" style must be examined. Throughout the eighteenth century, the stock European exotic musical language was the Turkish Style, which had achieved a huge popularity among lower-class audiences and the opera-going public alike. Such composers as Mozart and Haydn used it in a rather novel way: it is perhaps the first "standardized" tongue for exoticism. While certain gestures had been used to suggest "foreign" ideas in operas before the Turkish Style emerged (for example, open fifths, chantlike writing, or gibberish arias),[21] it was the first codified expression of the strange and exotic. The Turkish Style, with its repertoire of strange and somewhat crude musical gestures, made musical reference to the remote Turks, once feared but now mastered (in their absence!) through caricature and stereotype. This helped establish the precedent for the same process when the exotic group to which composers referred was the Gypsies.

CHAPTER 2

The Magyars, the Turks, the Siege of Vienna, and the Turkish Style

I

IN 1683 an invading force of Turks laid siege to the city of Vienna. In hindsight, this would assume mythic proportions as the last great East-West conflict, the historic showdown of Islam and Christendom. The sides, however, were not nearly so conveniently drawn up, nor were the causes leading up to the Siege of Vienna so uncomplicated. To be sure, the Turks were attempting a western expansion of their empire, and the Europeans were fighting in self-defense. But the "East" consisted not only of the Islamic Turks but also of the Christian Hungarians who were allied with them. The "West" involved in this struggle with the East hardly represented a monolithic entity, either: the Hapsburg principalities, feuding with each other on a more or less constant basis, formed an alliance with formerly peripheral Poland. Historically speaking, this was no more a clear-cut East-meets-West confrontation than the Crusades had been, but it did result in a final defeat for Turkish expansionism to the West.

From a musical perspective, the confrontation of the great powers at the walls of Vienna was the starting point for the "Turkish" musical craze that would take hold of Europe in the next century and that would be felt well into the nineteenth. It would also lay the cultural groundwork for the western reception of the *style hongrois*. Since Europeans were not accustomed to thinking much about the countries east of them, an epic battle that put Hungary center-stage served to arouse curiosity and interest in that country and everything associated with it. When the Gypsies later emerged from the suspect East playing Hungarian music and maintaining an apparent aloofness from society, reactions to them were in part conditioned by the aftereffects of the political and cultural upheaval surrounding the Siege.

The Hungarian lands had been strife torn and politically unstable for a considerable length of time before the crisis. The rival Turkish and Hapsburg empires fought for domination, but victories and territorial gains were temporary, losses were high, and Hungary remained a land divided. In general, Transylvania (in the east) and the western lands were Hapsburg controlled, and the Turks held sway over the central section. There was no strong centralized Hungarian government, and the Hungarian nobles had private armies, fortresses, and systems of taxation. The balance of power was therefore in a state of constant flux.

The populace, regardless of the ruling power, lived in a state of utter subjugation. Although the Magyar peasantry was Christian, the legacy of repressive Hapsburg overlordship had left it with little loyalty to political Christendom; in addition to mistreatment by the Turks, the peasants were plundered by both Hapsburg mercenaries and their own landlords. The Hungarian lands at this time were characterized by a lack of centralized power, stability, or even culture. Furthermore, this succession of rulers and political circumstances had left Hungary a country very much outside western orbits. The idea of a nobility proudly independent of central authority was alien to western Europeans. Even stranger was a peasantry clearly indifferent to whether it was ruled by Turks or Christians. These extraordinary cultural features left Hungary very much a question mark in the European mind.

A decade prior to the Turkish incursion, the status of both the Hungarians and their culture was at a low point. In addition to the usual hardships overlords traditionally visit on rural populations, Hungarian culture itself was repressed and persecuted in favor of the ruling German one. The Hapsburgs had designated German and Slavonic the national languages, for example, excluding Hungarian. It was under these oppressive circumstances that Imre Thököly, a young nobleman and Hungarian patriot, raised a force that became known as the *Kuruc*-warriors and mounted an armed struggle against Hapsburg rule.[1] While his revolt was successful, and resulted in the signing of a treaty in 1673, his power and leadership gradually declined from that point. Nonetheless, this uprising is still remembered as a time of patriotism and pride among Hungarians. As it was the nationalistic high point of the entire epoch, the musical language of the *Kuruc* period has a tremendous resonance for Hungarians. It echoes throughout later Hungarian music, colors the performance style of the Hungarian Gypsies, and accounts for the strong feeling of identification felt for this music by indigenous Magyars.

After 1673, Hapsburg rule had been pushed back, but Thököly was by no means ruling over a unified and stable political entity. Central government was still more a fiction than a reality. The Turks, continuing to hold large portions of Hungary and recognizing the stewardship of Thököly (they offered him "kingship" in 1682, which was refused), were therefore able to look westward from their empire and see a political circumstance of considerable instability, as well as a veritable open road to Vienna, the Hapsburg seat. The decline of Hapsburg authority meant, to the Turkish mind, that there was something of a power vacuum in the Hungarian lands. Hence, it represented an opportunity.

Turkish designs for the expansion of their empire had never been a secret in the West, and suspicious glances were frequently thrown eastward, not infrequently lighting on the Gypsies. Edward Brown, for example, describes the situation on entering Hungary just prior to 1673:

> Nor were we without fear also of *Gypsies,* who are stout and bold, and some of them have been noted Robbers. There are many of them in Hungaria, Servia, Bulgaria, and Macedonia; and some I saw at Larissa and other parts of Thessaly. They are in most towns and live by labour. . . . Though they be remotely dispersed, yet they are thought to have their beginning about Wallachia, and the adjoining parts, many of them conceived to be spies unto the *Turk.* A little before I came to *Leopoldstadt,* by *Freystadt,* a great drove of them appeared in those parts; which the people suspected to be Spies of the *Visier* of *Buda,* to take notice of the state of those parts, and how that Fort proceeded.[2]

This testimony highlights several interesting things. The association of Gypsy with Turk is an important one, and it will have a musical resonance when the Turkish Style is first mixed with and then eclipsed by the *style hongrois.* Moreover, in the seventeenth century we can see the Gypsy already being connected, in the European mind, with the East in general and suspected of readiness to ally with the Heathen against the Christian world (as, for example, the Hungarians were seen to do). Incidentally, this suspicion survived long after the Siege and is even more explicitly stated in a German encyclopedia of 1749, which speaks of "believable indications that [the Gypsies] are informers, traitors, and spies . . . in the

Christian countries for the Turks and other enemies of Christendom."[3] The societal view of the Gypsies as essentially separate from and foreign to any indigenous population is also apparent here, and this idea, even despite attempts at this time to settle and forcibly assimilate the Gypsies in Hungary, would remain fixed in the popular mind.

Leaving the Gypsies aside, Brown says further on that many locals suspected that the Turk would again try his hand at Vienna,[4] and he comments on the cruel conditions under which the Turks forced the Hungarians to live in the areas they controlled.[5] There were no illusions on either point: the Turks would return, and as overlords they had been no kinder than the Hapsburgs or Hungarian nobles themselves; excesses of hardship sometimes drove entire villages to pick up and move *en masse* to avoid further abuse, and the Magyars had to bear such losses without repayment.[6]

Even as fellow members of Christendom and as brethren suffering under the Turkish yoke, Magyars themselves were viewed with distrust by Hapsburgs and other western Europeans. Dealings with those who were still under Hapsburg domination did not proceed in the businesslike fashion the Hapsburgs were used to expecting. Thomas Barker quotes a diplomatic complaint dating from some years before the *Kuruc* uprising, first offering some historical background:

> Of course, one would not be granting the Hapsburgs their historical due if one were to assume that the estates—a body hardly representative of the whole Hungarian nation—were composed of particularly rational or amendable individuals. Apparently, many a great lord was not only chivalrous, dashing, and patriotic, but also fickle, unpredictable, and completely callous toward his peasant fellow countrymen. One seemingly unprejudiced observer of the latter seventeenth century wrote:
>
> "The Hungarians make their laws energetically but

do not hold to them. Every magnate could call himself a little king because he treats his subjects like slaves. The nobles, who disregard their own laws, paradoxically insist that their King observe them. They want him to be their protector but not their lord. They say openly that their freedom does not go well with the status of being a subject."[7]

"While such claims are difficult to substantiate objectively," Barker continues, "they are still worth noting, for many other foreigners and certain natives have also maintained that the Magyars are among the world's more ungovernable peoples."[8]

Also well known to Europe were the Magyars' origins as an aggregate of nomadic, equestrian tribes from the East. This history was wholly different from those of their western neighbors, and certainly contributed to their image as a race apart and of an entirely different character. When this history was combined with testimony such as Molin's, a European view of them as headstrong and unfathomable was unavoidable.

Furthermore, by the time the Turks marched toward Vienna in the summer of 1683 (the Siege proper began in July), Imre Thököly had already concluded a treaty with them, which he honored only insofar as it meant he did not ally with the Hapsburgs. Rather than helping the Turks, he ended up withholding military support at a crucial point in the struggle, thereby sealing the ultimate doom of their effort. Nonetheless, his "treaty" only cemented the image of the Magyar as somehow not-quite-Christian, answerable to alien, eastern loyalties and quite probably untrustworthy. In fact, Magyars were assumed to have precisely those qualities that later would be attributed to the Romani Gypsies who came westward from their country, playing their music. The distrust already felt for the Magyars would come to be associated with anything emerging from the east, Hungarian or otherwise.

Returning to the Siege itself, at the walls of Vienna things initially looked hopeful for the Turks, and their musicians played every morning and evening. Indeed, part of the Janissaries' regimen involved music played throughout the course of battle, since without music the soldiers might falter.[9] The instruments were primarily percussive, being varieties of cymbals and drums, while the horns they were described as playing had only one or two notes to contribute, not a whole melody. The noise level increased on July 31, when the Christian musicians were ordered to play while the Turks were doing the same thing, with the battle raging all the while and with each side registering scorn for the music of the other.[10] This *ancien régime* battle-of-the-bands seems to have established the reputation for the noisemaking, jangling inferiority of the Turkish music in the European mind once and for all. The Turkish musicians making a racket (to the European mind, at least) outside the walls of Vienna proved to be an unforgettable image of besieged Christendom, and it lingered in the popular imagination for more than a century.

The course and outcome of the battle are the province of history books: the indecisiveness of the Hapsburg command, the worsening conditions within the walls of Vienna, the eleventh-hour rescue by King John Sobieski of Poland and his forces, and the defeat and ultimate rout of the Turks. Following the final confrontation, it should be added, Sobieski felt it advisable to conclude a treaty with Thököly and the Magyars, who (while ostensibly Turkish allies) had withheld support and were, after all, still Christian. The Hungarians thus were accepted back into the western fold almost immediately, at least in political if not cultural terms. What is important for our purposes is the cultural legacy of this historic episode: European contempt for the Turks, feelings of strangeness and mistrust for the Hungarians and the Gypsies (the latter not least because they emerged from the country of the former), and a memory of percussive Turkish battle music which would later become a craze.

II

It would be a mistake to imagine that the rout of the Turks in 1683 marked an end to European apprehensions. In addition to the memories of the Ottomans as a constant threat and conquering military power, the huge cultural disparity between East and West continued to provoke feelings of mistrust and insecurity. Indeed, William Hunter, an English barrister travelling in 1792, stated that in Moldavia and Wallachia (north of Hungary, east of the German Lands) Turks were still more feared than Germans or Russians.[11] Throughout the eighteenth century, the major power east of Vienna still produced, in addition to amusement and condescension, some insecurity in the western mind.

The stereotype of the Turk was the subliminal message conveyed to the listener whenever the so-called Turkish Style, popularized in operas based on Turkish subjects and later in instrumental music, was heard. Such operas were highly successful; the popular image of the Turk represented in them centered on promiscuous sexuality (the European interpretation of Islamic polygamy) and violence. As Thomas Bauman points out, however, these operas appeared at the same time that Enlightenment writers were creating heroes from the east who did not resemble this stereotype at all.[12] Certainly, one standard form of social criticism has always been to create ideal types of another culture so as to present them in contrast with the social ills of one's own time and place. But the Turk in European opera seems also to have filled the ever-present need for an "other," an outsider with both positive and negative qualities, which would later be filled in popular culture at large by the Gypsies.

The reviled and supposedly Turkish tendency to promiscuity would traditionally have been represented onstage by a harem; the Turkish propensity to violence suggested by horrible threats offered by Turkish characters.[13] Both carried a sense of the forbidden (and perhaps also the coveted) in a socially restricted Europe. Once these ideas were established, the typical operatic drama would likely involve the unsuccessful attempts of the Turk to subjugate a European female to proper harem submissiveness and the civilizing of the Turk through learned Western behavior, perhaps involving proper wooing procedure.[14] The range of behaviors (from noble to repulsive, threatening to humorous, enviable to contemptible) usually associated with Islamic society could thus be used in creating colorful tales of distant lands, in supporting the use of a popular musical language, and for reinforcing mixed but still simplistic stereotypes of the inhabitants of those lands, and of lands to the east in general. Of course, we will soon encounter the exaggerated positive-negative Gypsy stereotype; its parallel with that of the Turks is almost exact. In any case, a study of the Turkish Style tells us more about Europeans than about Turks, and this pattern, too, will remain with the *style hongrois*.

The primary musical characteristics associated with the Turkish Style in Europe are percussive. Miriam Karpilow Whaples quotes the English traveller Dr. John Covel, who heard the Turkish musicians play in the late seventeenth century. According to Dr. Covel,

> 1st there are trumpets, which come in onely now and then to squeel out a loud note or two, but never play a whole tune. 2d, pipers—their pipe is much the same with our trebble shaume or Hooboy [oboe]; these play continually without any pause. 3rd, great drums, but not bract [Whaples gives the definition "metal-plated"] as ours, nor corded at the bottom; they beat them at both ends, the top with the right hand with a great stick

at every long or leading note, the bottom with a little in their left hand at every small or passing note; these have their pauses often. 4thly, little kettle or dish drums (for they have both) dissonant one to the other, for they are in paires; these rest sometime likewise. 5thly they have 2 brasse platters about a foote wide, which they hang loose in their hands, and clatter them one against the other.

I am very inclinable to believe all this Musick old, and mention'd in Scripture. These last either [*sic*] were the cymbals mention'd in Chron. 15, 19.[15]

Noteworthy is the fact that while two possible melody instruments are mentioned, the trumpet and the pipe, the former is described as playing a note or two without offering a full tune, and the pipe plays incessantly—again with no mention of a tune, although there may have been something tunelike in the music it incessantly played. One imagines an energetic and aggressive noise, with metric regularity and a strong and irresistible beat, which could certainly spur troops to extraordinary physical deeds. There is no implication that this was ever Turkish art music, of course; as battle music, it had an explicit purpose.

Perhaps not surprisingly, most of the percussion instruments used in Europe's art music were brought into service for the Turkish Style. In symphonic and operatic uses, prominent percussion was the most noteworthy characteristic. There evolved the so-called *batterie turque,* which consisted of cymbals, tambourine, triangle, and bass drum, although the triangle, having no eastern analog, is a strictly western addition.[16] Example 1 gives an excerpt from Haydn's Symphony no. 100, which shows how a variant (tympani rather than a tambourine) of the *batterie turque* might be deployed in symphonic usage. We will see that other features contained in the excerpt, such as the minor key and the simple marchlike writing, are also standard fare in the Turkish Style.

Example 1. Turkish percussion. Haydn, Symphony no. 100, II, mm. 57–61.

In addition to literal use of percussion, a body of musical gestures evolved that amounted to a "Turkish" musical dialect within the standard eighteenth-century vocabulary. Both Whaples and Bauman list these characteristics; I do so again here for convenient reference. The roles of the Turkish Style as a language of lighter, more popular music, as a dialect that refers to the cultural stereotype of the Other, and as a widely understood musical designation of the exotic all have parallels in the *style hongrois*. The Turkish Style provides, therefore, important background for our study.

One characteristic of the Turkish Style is the prominent

and stark melodic use of the interval of the third, sometimes alternated with the fifth. Example 2a gives the closing measures of Mozart's *Rondo alla turca* (the third movement of the piano sonata K. 331 in A major), and 2b gives the opening vocal line from the Janissary Chorus from Act I of the *Abduction*. It is impossible to miss the crude way in which these intervals are repeated and emphasized in a way wholly different from non-"Turkish" pieces and distinct from accepted practice.

Despite their frequent deployment in the Turkish Style, there is no mention of thirds or fifths in the descriptions of those who heard the Janissaries play at the walls of Vienna. My own suspicion is that the third was a widely accepted compositional solution to the question unconsciously placed by John Covel's description: if the Turks' trumpets played only two notes and could not really play a melody, which two would they be and how would they relate to one another? Not only could the third fit neatly into European triadic harmonic practice, it could be used in a stylized fanfare-melody of the sort that might be appropriate to a military scene. It could be loud, shrieky, and percussive, in other words, but it was also more flexible than any other single interval would be. The fifth, of course, was the result of simply stacking a pair of thirds.

Interestingly, Bence Szabolcsi has noted the similarity of the stressed melodic third to figures common in the *"Törö-kös,"* a dance whose name means "in the Turkish Style" and that appears in the folk repertories of certain lowland Hungarian villages.[17] He felt that such dances seem to preserve genuine Turkish march tunes, and he also points out that Gypsies travelling east could well have borne these tunes into the Viennese orbit. This seems particularly credible when we remember the long years of Turkish occupation, during which Hungarian exposure to Turkish marching tunes would

Example 2. Stark use of thirds.

2a. Mozart, Sonata in A Major, K. 331, III *(Rondo alla turca)*, closing.

2b. Mozart, *Abduction from the Seraglio,* Janissary Chorus from Act I *(Singt dem grossen Bassa Lieder),* opening vocal line.

have been not only possible but unavoidable. Szabolcsi's examples are full of rebounding thirds similar to the Mozart excerpt in example 2a; if the *Törökös* in fact reflects genuine Turkish music, this would suggest very strongly that the "one or two notes" supposedly played by the Turkish trumpets would indeed have involved the interval of a third.

Other arresting aspects in example 2b include the raised fourths and the parallel octaves. As Bauman points out, the so-called Lydian (raised) fourth is also used by Gluck in his opera *La Rencontre imprévue* (see example 3).[18] While this interval will also become part of the *style hongrois,* in that context it will most often result from an inflection, an augmented second above the third degree of the minor scale, rather than from a true Lydian fifth, which consists of three consecutive whole steps above the prime (producing a raised fourth) and a half step below the fifth degree. The parallel octaves, which could be produced by merely having a vocal part double the bass line, are particularly interesting; certain travellers said that Turkish music was played in unisons or octaves, so they might be no more than faithful representations.[19] But these octaves also hearken back to the pre-"Turkish," seventeenth-century operatic exotica of André Campra and Jean-Baptiste Lully, which was a sort of panforeign group of inflections that could suggest any distant locale: the Indies, America, or Provence. Given the attractiveness of distant, fantastic realms in operatic culture, Mozart's musical materials might well descend from sources more disparate than standard eighteenth-century *turquerie.*

Another feature of the Turkish Style is the meter, 2/4, with a pounding, even eighth-note rhythm. Both the Janissary Chorus and the piano sonata excerpted above feature this, as does nearly every other example of Turkish music. (The Haydn excerpt above is an exception, although it could easily

Example 3. The Lydian fourth. Gluck, *La Rencontre imprévue,*
Overture, opening.

have been barred in 2/4.) According to the theorist Christian
Schubart,

> It [succeeds best] in 2/4 meter, however many at-
> tempts with other meters have been made. No other
> genre of music requires such a firm, decided, and over-
> poweringly predominant beat. The first beat of each
> measure is so strongly marked with a new and manly
> accent that it is virtually impossible to get out of step.[20]

Thus, metrical practice in the Turkish Style resembles the
intervallic usage in that it ranges from the merely obvious to
the openly crude.

Repeated notes in both melody and accompaniment are
also common features of the Turkish Style. Indeed, repeated
accompaniment notes are present in every musical example
for this chapter excepting the Haydn, which is the only one
with actual percussion instruments. Examples 4a and 4b give
examples of repetition in the melody: 4a gives the opening of
Beethoven's "Turkish March" from the *Ruins of Athens;* 4b
gives the first four measures of Mozart's Sonata in A minor,
K. 310. Again, the percussive quality of the writing is in both
cases its most distinctive feature. The martial mood conveyed
by both the simple harmonies and the repetitive tattoo can be
seen to make a convincing replacement for literal percussion.

Even more literally depictive of percussion are the grace
notes and other jangling ornaments, which are ubiquitous in

Example 4. Melodic repeated notes.

4a. Beethoven, *Ruins of Athens,* "Turkish March" (reduction).

4b. Mozart, Sonta in A Minor, K. 310, I, mm. 1–4.

the Turkish Style (and will also appear in the *style hongrois).* This feature is evident in examples 4a and 4b, as well as in example 5, which gives the opening of the *Rondo alla turca.* The repeated notes in the accompaniment and the importance of the third and fifth in the melody are also very much present.

Still another device evoking Turkish "crudity" is the harmonic stasis and tendency toward blunt and inelegant harmonic practice shown in all the examples thus far. As with several of the other devices in the Turkish Style, harmonic usage sometimes borders on the gauche. A characteristic, nonfunctional harmonic deployment will appear in the *style hongrois,* in which context it may represent either musical ignorance or the faithful reproduction of the performance style, but there it rarely exhibits the crudity of the Turkish type.

An interesting rhythmic device is the opening of a section with long note values in the melody, immediately followed by much shorter diminutions. Example 2b, from the Janissary Chorus, shows this procedure, as does example 3, the

Example 5. Noisy ornaments. Mozart, Sonata in A Major, K. 331, III *(Rondo alla turca),* opening.

beginning of Gluck's opera overture. There seems to be nothing specifically "Turkish" about this, but its jarring, noisy effect fits the same pattern of all the other characteristics seen so far.

One further gesture cited by Bauman and Whaples is the addition of upper neighbor notes to descending scale passages in the form of escape tones. This lends an additional shaking, noisemaking effect and can be seen in example 6, the opening of the final Janissary chorus from the *Abduction.* Bar 9 shows this feature, and the excerpt itself also contains a pounding 2/4 meter, repeated notes in melody and accompaniment, a long note value followed by short ones, and parallel octaves— a veritable "Turkish" cornucopia.

I would expand the definition of this final (and appropriately noisy) gesture to include any motoric, noisy sixteenth-note passagework figure. The Mozart piano sonata movements are full of it, as is the Haydn Trio movement to be examined in the next chapter. I see all these gestures as ultimately being derived from the time-honored "wrong-note" principle of musical exoticism, which was never limited to the Turkish Style: what our *good* music does not favor or

Example 6. Descending passage of escape tones. Mozart, *Abduction from the Seraglio,* final chorus from Act II, introduction reduction.

encourage, their (whoever "they" might be, depending on epoch, context, or opera plot) *crude* music probably does, or may as well do. This principle is the common thread running through the pounding 2/4, the harmonic dullness, the repeated notes, incessant thirds and fifths, and jangling passage-work. It produced a kind of stylized noisemaking that was in direct opposition to everything a delightful, elegant piece of European music was supposed to be. Reports from the walls of Vienna aside, Europe would still have had no trouble attributing this sort of music to the distant Turks.

Given the noisy, percussive quality of the Turkish Style, for all its suggestiveness it must have seemed very far from the prevailing musical aesthetic of the time. In a famous letter of September 26, 1781, Mozart discusses certain issues involved in composing the *Abduction:*

> The passions, be they powerful or not, must never be expressed to the point of disgust, and music, even in the most horrifying situation, must never offend the ear, but must actually please, and consequently remain music.[21]

The fact that the Turkish Style frequently bordered on the gauche and ugly would certainly have contributed to its exotic and peculiar associations. In the case of Mozart, it may even have been a bit of an aesthetic strain, given his belief that to remain music something must please the ear and never offend. The radically different and comparatively crude sound of the Turkish Style amounts to a different type of music altogether, something between dialect (for which the body of "Turkish" gestures is really insufficient) and sound effects.

Above all, the one historical aspect of the Turkish Style that must be stressed is its popularity, and not only with the opera-going part of the public. Instrumental music, such as the Mozart sonata movements cited above, appeared and capitalized on the popularity of the opera. Pianofortes began to appear with "Turkish" stops that would activate bells, chimes, and percussive devices to create maximum racket while playing. The urban bourgeois taste, therefore, ran strongly in that direction also. Louis Spohr, travelling through Europe in the year 1802, described a situation at Hohenzirze in which the festivities celebrating the crown prince's birthday involved Janissary music being played for the peasants, while dance music would be provided for the townspeople later.[22] Even the lower classes, it seems, had a taste for the Turkish Style.

Indeed, one gets the impression of a phenomenon in some ways similar to rock and roll. The cultural implications of the Turkish Style were slightly alien, forbidden, and certainly earthy. The music was percussive, far less complex than the prevailing musical style of the time, and so immediately elemental and accessible that all strata of society might respond to it on a visceral level. Like the rock and roll rhythm section (electric guitar-electric bass-drums) that now accompanies everything from easy listening music to musical theater, even the instruments the Turkish Style required would become far more common as a result of its dissemination: Carl Maria von Weber, for example, would take the presence of the "Turkish Music" (meaning the instruments that played it) for granted in writing about orchestral logistics in the theater, and the abovementioned Turkish stops on pianos testify to its influence in the sphere of domestic music making.

Many aspects of the Turkish Style were shared by the *style hongrois:* great popularity, dubious cultural associations, and an elemental attraction that made it successful with all levels of society. As the *style hongrois* superceded the Turkish Style as Europe's common exotic musical dialect, there was a period of time during which the two styles coexisted. Indeed, characteristics of both were mixed freely, although it is by no means clear that they were confused, or understood as part of the same exotic complex, as at least one writer has suggested. But it is Mozart, Haydn, and Beethoven, all of whom used the Turkish Style with complete command and assurance, who also pioneered the use of the *style hongrois* and its assimilation into art music.

This is not to deny the contributions to the development of the *style hongrois* made by such composers as Weber (who also used the Turkish Style), Hummel, and numerous minor figures; it is simply to point out that the three most influential composers of the late eighteenth and early nineteenth centuries understood both exotic styles, and while they could blend them they could also, even in this nascent period for the *style hongrois,* use them as completely discrete dialects. They would even use explicit title designations such as *alla turca* or *all' Ingharese.* Such a title (or subtitle), I should add, was no guarantee that the piece would be purely Turkish or purely Hungarian, but it does suggest that the composers were aware of both.

This Turkish-to-Gypsy transitional period, extending

roughly from the last quarter of the eighteenth century into the second decade of the nineteenth, is interesting in the way it parallels other music transitions taking place at the same time: the expansion of the eighteenth-century musical vocabulary, the transition from the notion of affect to the Romantic notion of pure feeling, and the evolution of the harmonic language. The quaint, stylized associations with the Turks were also fading and being replaced (as we will see in chapter 4) by the fearsome yet alluring reputation of the Gypsies. The *style hongrois,* therefore, would speak to the emerging Romantic sensibility with an immediacy and relevance unavailable to the largely burlesque Turkish Style.

CHAPTER 3

The Emergence of the
Style Hongrois

ALMOST FROM the earliest appearance of the Turkish Style, Hungarian-Gypsy and other central European elements began to be combined with it in a rather free mixture of exotic musical gestures. The reasons for this were not exclusively musical: cultural associations with the distant but threatening East were at least as relevant as the stylistic compatibility of these not-wholly-Western musics. As we saw in chapter 2, concurrent with worries about the Turks and their geopolitical role, a cultural consciousness concerning the Gypsies was beginning to emerge. Not only was embattled Vienna the eastern outpost of western Europe, it had also been a center for western-migrating Gypsies since the time of the Siege, and the reputation of the Gypsy musicians there waxed markedly. Predictably, then, it is in the music of the Classical

It will be necessary to cite and discuss individual gestures of the *style hongrois* in this chapter. A brief explanation will accompany each new term, but a full discussion of the gestures, their origins, and their deployment is contained in chapter 5.

composers of the Viennese orbit that the various manifestations of "eastern" music began to meet and combine both with each other and with the conventional musical language.

One early and obvious example of this blend is the overture to Gluck's opera *Le Rencontre imprévue* (1764). One passage from this piece was discussed in chapter 2, and another is shown in example 7. Here, Gluck mixes stock Turkish elements with the *Kuruc*-fourth, a fanfare-like Hungarian figure that rebounds between the fifth scale degree and the upper prime and that dates from and is associated with the *Kuruc* period. One happy aspect of this figure is the way that, when metered, it closely resembles and complements the ubiquitous rebounding thirds and fifths of the Turkish style and so assimilates easily into the "Turkish" texture.

Example 7. Gluck, *Le Rencontre imprévue*, Overture, mm. 19–25.

Haydn illustrates the subtler ways in which these musics could interrelate. Born in 1732 in eastern Austria near the Hungarian border, he was exposed to both German and Hungarian culture throughout his life. He spent his youth (after age eight) and early adulthood in Vienna, singing as a choirboy at the Cathedral of St. Stephen and later living in precarious circumstances, working at odd jobs, giving music lessons, and studying Fux's counterpoint treatise. After a short period of service with a Bohemian nobleman, he took a position in 1761 (which he would hold for thirty years) with Prince Paul Anton Esterházy, who spent much of the year with his court in the country estate of Esterháza, in the Hungarian countryside. Beyond a doubt, Haydn's exposure to the musical languages of the various peoples of these districts offered him a far wider palette of source musics than would have been available to composers based further west.

Bence Szabolcsi went so far as to suggest that "it is increasingly obvious that for Haydn and his contemporaries Slavonic, Gypsy, Rumanian and Turkish music formed one single—mixed but scarcely divisible—complex."[1] This may be a slight overstatement. We will see that in many cases the styles do appear to be mixed. Nonetheless, that Haydn understood Turkish and Hungarian-Gypsy musics as separate entities is unquestionably proven by the thoroughly Turkish second movement of his Symphony no. 100, discussed in chapter 2, and by an undiluted Gypsy essay such as the second movement of String Quartet op. 54/2, an improvisatory Gypsy lament (see example 8). The use of Turkish music in the "military" symphony needed no additional Gypsy flavoring, while any Turkish coloring would have been irrelevant to the Gypsy fiddle display of the string quartet (to my knowledge, the first example of the *hallgató* style to appear in Viennese music).

This aside, Szabolcsi's observation does point to the fact that, understood to be discrete entities or not, these musics were not always treated independently either by Haydn or by other composers of the time. Haydn's *Rondo all' Ungherese,* the finale to the D major keyboard concerto (1767?), is a well-known instance of the sort of hybrid Szablocsi means: despite its title, it has more Turkish elements than Hungarian-Gypsy ones, and the Hungarian presence is largely limited to the

Example 8. Haydn, String Quartet, op. 54/2, II, mm. 9–12.

Kuruc-fourth. However, there are also more complex and subtle Haydnesque blends.

The finale to his Piano Trio in G Major, Hob. XV:25 (Rondo, "In the Gipsies' style"), is a thoroughgoing mixture of Turkish and Gypsy elements.[2] The Hungarian-Gypsy identification is established by Haydn's own mood or performance indication, but the opening figure is identifiably "Turkish": it is a rondo theme made up of descending broken thirds and realized in a particularly noisy and jangling fashion (example 9a). The motoric, sequential writing continues to measure 35, where the piano's percussive left hand and parallel thirds in the right hand accompany a violin figure based on the traditional *alla turca* upper-neighbor ornaments (example 9b). Syncopations begin to creep in, however, and by mm. 67–70 (example 9c) we are in parallel minor; while the piano part still looks somewhat "Turkish," the cello is maintaining a low drone and the violin has prominent syncopated double stops (the rhythmic figure here is the *alla zoppa,* or "limping" rhythm—both this and the low drone will become standard gestures of the *style hongrois).* Measures 83–88 (example 9d) are even more stereotypically Hungarian in that they form a truncated (six-bar) phrase, maintain the *alla zoppa* rhythm, and feature a pizzicato (plucked, as opposed to bowed) figure in the violin. Pizzicato, as we will see in chapter 5, had been understood to be a Gypsy violin technique since the 1780s at least.

Example 9. Turkish and Gypsy elements. Haydn, Piano Trio, Hob. XV:25, III ("Rondo, in the Gipsies' style").

9a. Opening.

An even more intriguing piece is the second movement of Haydn's Symphony no. 103, the "Drum Roll." This movement resembles an étude in paneastern exoticism, cast in the form of a set of variations in alternating major and minor

9b. Mm. 35–42.

modes. It contains many Hungarian-Gypsy gestures that seem almost methodically set out: these include the raised fourth (associated with the augmented seconds of the so-called Gypsy scale, but which can also appear in major mode; we also saw the raised fourth used in a Turkish context by Gluck); characteristic Hungarian rhythms (anapests,[3] dotted rhythm à la *verbunkos);* and soloistic treatments of instruments associated with Gypsies (violin, oboe). Some excerpts from this curious movement are shown in examples 10a–c. The timpani, which make their appearance late in the movement, must serve to represent some kind of Turkish presence, although the influences in this movement do seem to be predominantly those of the *style hongrois.*

9c. Mm. 67–70.

9d. Mm. 83–88.

Example 10. Exoticisms. Haydn, Symphony no. 103, II.

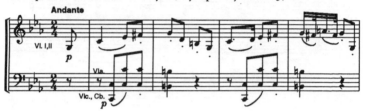

10a. Mm. 1–4: augmented seconds, dotted rhythms.

10b. Mm. 39–40: accented anapests.

10c. Mm. 85–88: Lydian fourth, soloistic violin triplets.

Mozart, somewhat younger than Haydn but very much an artistic contemporary, also used "Turkish" and Hungarian-Gypsy musics both separately and simultaneously. As we saw in chapter 2, the Turkish idiom formed the basis of one of his operas and of several instrumental works, and he used it with as much assurance as any of his contemporaries. His forays into the *style hongrois,* however, do not have quite the confidence of Haydn's, which is not surprising; his birthplace (Salzburg) was not as far east, and he never had the regular lengthy stays in Hungary that Haydn did. He also could produce a stylized *ongherese* such as the last movement of the String Quartet in F Major, K. 590, although he does not give it that explicit appellation. The unique Mozartean elegance stands in place of Haydnesque vividness and immediacy: some of the rawer elements are curbed, but such features as virtuosic violin writing, *alla zoppa* syncopations, drones in the lower strings, and brusque harmonic shifts (such as the jerk from C to D-flat major over the double bar), are still very much in evidence (see example 11).

A much-noted "exotic" work of Mozart, the third movement of the Violin Concerto in A Major, K. 219 (sometimes subtitled the "Turkish"), blends the two styles. This minuet-finale begins and ends in A major, but its lengthy middle section (itself in ABA' form) seems to come from a different musical universe.[4] As Szabolcsi observed, the solo violin figure beginning in m. 134 is a clear evocation of Hungarian-Gypsy writing;[5] it even features the familiar *Kuruc*-fourth in the fourth bar (see example 12a). However, this episode's middle section, which begins in m. 164, is replete with stock Turkish features: the meter is a thumping 2/4, it is initially harmonically static, and ornaments and exaggerated dynamic effects are used to imitate percussion (see example 12b). Szabolcsi identifies a Dittersdorf melody and the fragments of an earlier ballet of Mozart (which themselves reflect central European dance music, not *turcquerie)* as antecedents of this movement.[6] This serves to illustrate not only the way in which source musics were beginning to be mixed and matched in larger-scale pieces, but also the way vernacular and folk musics in general were beginning to exceed their time-honored social limits and roles.

Example 11. Mozart, String Quartet in F Major, K. 590, IV, mm. 125–38.

Example 12. Mozart, Violin Concerto in A Major, K. 219, "Turkish," III.

12a. Mm. 132–37.

Beethoven, sometime student of Haydn and an admirer of Mozart, seems to have followed their established pattern, using the two styles in tandem as well as separately. He was not only completely at home with traditional *turcquerie* (e.g., his famous Turkish marches from the *Ruins of Athens* and Symphony no. 9), but was also clearly aware of the emergent Hungarian-Gypsy style; according to Julius Kaldy, student and popularizer of old Hungarian music, Beethoven heard performances of the renowned Gypsy violinist János Bihari "often and with pleasure."[7] One little-known but clear ex-

12b. Mm. 164–72.

ample of Beethoven's use of the *style hongrois* is the little
Gypsy march he inserted into the third movement of his
adolescent piano concerto in E-flat, written in 1784 (see
example 13). This passage is in the parallel minor, shows
prominent dotted rhythms and ornaments, and uses the
quintessentially Gypsy augmented second in m. 165. A more
famous example of Beethoven's use of the *style hongrois* is the
verbunkos-type theme from the final movement of the *Eroica*
symphony; his clearest use of the idiom, however, is the

Example 13. Beethoven, Piano Concerto in E-flat Major (1784), III, mm. 161–68.

overture to *King Stephen*, which uses Gypsy syncopations and other inflections to suggest the Hungarian setting of the play.[8] A less remarked-upon instance is the finale of String Quartet op. 18/4: the excerpt given in example 14 is the minor mode, and features Gypsy-type dance figures and characteristic *alla zoppa* syncopations.

Beethoven's well-known *Alla Ingharese* (better known by the probably spurious nickname, "Rage over a Lost Penny") illustrates his manner of blending the two styles. This piece is explicitly linked to the Hungarian-Gypsy tradition by its title, but its musical materials seem at least as closely related to the Turkish Style. Example 15a gives the opening four measures: the crude right-hand figure, made up of an arpeggiated chord and a jangling ornament, is accompanied by a thoroughly "Turkish" left-hand part consisting of repeated

Example 14. Beethoven, String Quartet in C Minor, op. 18/4, IV, mm. 163–65.

percussive chords that maintain the root pitch even when the harmony changes to the dominant in the third measure (all of this, of course, in 2/4 meter). As this is the rondo theme of the piece, the Turkish style returns several times, alternated with such "Hungarian" passages as that shown in example 15b: relative minor, *alla zoppa* syncopation, virtuoso violin-type figure in the right hand. Example 15c gives the end of one strophe and the beginning of another: the first section closes with characteristic Hungarian anapests in mm. 109–10, there is a sudden and unprepared harmony change from G major to E major, and the new tune opens with another common Hungarian rhythm, the spondee.

It is clear from these examples that while the Turkish style and the *style hongrois* were understood as separate entities and could be used as such, at least as often they were combined in an undifferentiated mix. One possible reason for the coexistence of the styles in works of this epoch may be provided by the subtitle of Haydn's Trio finale, discussed above ("in the Gipsies' style"). As was pointed out in chapter

Example 15. Beethoven, *Alla Ingharese* ("Rage over a Lost Penny").

15a. Mm. 1–4.

15b. Mm. 25–28.

15c. Mm. 109–14.

1, the Gypsies were understood to be Hungary's professional musicians, suggesting that as entertainers they played many types of music, not solely their own. Contemporary descriptions, for example, have them playing court dances such as the minuet and a selection called the "French March."[9] Further, as outlined in chapter 2, the Turkish Style was not a style limited to isolated operas and dramatic presentations: pianofortes were being manufactured with "Turkish" stops, and Spohr's testimony suggested that Turkish music was popular with even the lowest classes of society. Thus, such exotic "blends" as we have seen in Haydn, Mozart, and Beethoven might also be interpreted as no blends at all; rather, they may be stylized but fairly straightforward representations of Gypsy performances. People liked (and paid for) Turkish music, so the Gypsies could well have played it. Some of their own performance "accent" would certainly have gotten mixed in, but not with any particular artistic agenda in mind.

Somewhat more distant from the Viennese Gypsy-Turkish musical matrix is the opera *Die Zigeuner* by the Bonn-based Christian Gottlob Neefe, who is best remembered as one of Beethoven's teachers.[10] Written in 1777 to a libretto by H. S. Möller, the opera indicates that Neefe was at least aware of the Gypsies as a cultural phenomenon, although there seems to be no effort to evoke their music in any systematic way. Certain aspects of the *style hongrois* do appear here, but in such feeble concentrations that it seems coincidental, and they are accompanied by a great deal of other random exoticism. This work may be the last gasp of the Baroque "different = exotic" approach to operatic musical language.

Neefe represents the Gypsies with far more pieces in triple meter (a relative rarity in the *style hongrois)* than might seem appropriate: not only do mazurkalike 3/4 meters occur, but faster 3/8 pieces as well. The Gypsy spirit seems to be represented by occasional rhythmic inflections such as characteristic syncopations, sequences of ornamental triplets (such as we saw in Haydn's Symphony no. 103) and Lombard (accented short-long) rhythms. Most curious, as I am not the first to observe, is the fact that *Die Zigeuner* has no numbers

in the minor mode at all.[11] This seems surprising, given that
minor mode is generally a *conditio sine qua non* of the mature
style hongrois, and that minor was already long associated
with Hungarian and eastern musics in general,[12] but Neefe
seems not to have felt its presence necessary to a Gypsy opera.
As might also be concluded from the free and easy "Turkish"-
Gypsy mixes, pleasing the popular palate was a far more
relevant consideration than was any kind of stylistic authenticity.

But the Hungarian-Gypsy vernacular was becoming highly
attractive to the public in its purer forms. This is made
apparent by the many pieces in this style published with the
amateur market in mind. Arrangements of *verbunkos* intended
for domestic use, mostly for piano, began appearing in
Vienna in 1784, under such titles as *Ungarischer tanz* and
Hongraise, and thereafter continued to appear in great number.[13] (As a matter of fact, the *style hongrois* continued to
flourish in this repertoire well into the twentieth century,
long after it had ceased to be a viable language in art music.)
The profusion of such *Hausmusik* using the *style hongrois*
attests to the style's commerical viability, the breadth of its
dissemination, and the increasing awareness of things musically Hungarian. When we in the twentieth century identify
Hungarian gestures in the works of Haydn, Mozart, and
Beethoven we need not doubt that audiences of the time
would have understood them as such; there was an entire
body of amateur musical literature that made the connection
for them. The Hungarian Gypsies were, as they departed
Hungary, increasingly prevalent as providers of cafe entertainment, so this dialect could only have been understood as
the Gypsies' musical language.

These works show the *style hongrois* to be well known to
the musical public at a very early date. This is particularly
important, as it has generally been assumed, in recent times,

that such purely Hungarian-Gypsy utterances were a product of the Romantic sensibility, first appearing in the works of Liszt and Brahms, or at earliest with Schubert. This genre of *Hausmusik,* however, demonstrates a strong presence of such music in the public mind and ear at the height of the Classical era.

In fact, it is precisely at this time that the organist, composer, and writer Christian Schubart acknowledged a characteristic Hungarian style in his *Ideen zu einer Ästhetik der Tonkunst* (written while he was imprisoned in Hohenasperg in 1784–1785), and his description clearly refers to the same kind of music we have been seeing:

> The Hungarian Dance has several original figures, and the Heyducks have melodies so original they rather approach the Gypsies' dances. The meter is always 2/4, the tempo more slow than fast, and as far as modulation it is totally bizarre: for example, it can begin with four measures in G and then finish in C; and so have many eccentric turns. This dance does very well when used in the theater.[14]

Idiomatic figures, duple meter, and a wild, unpredictable harmonic vocabulary are prominent elements of the *style hongrois*. It is interesting, by the way, that he ascribes this music to the Heyducks, rebellious Hungarian peasants and farmers from the previous century who ended up as mercenaries after losing their land. In the Prussian dialect, "Heidemak" was a highly uncomplimentary term,[15] and this, as well as the reference to the Gypsies, may suggest how little respect Schubart had for such "bizarre" music.

In general terms, the difference between the deployment of the *style hongrois* in the eighteenth and nineteenth centuries can be summarized this way: In the eighteenth century, the vernacular's rough edges were for the most part softened in the interest of the homogeneity of musical language (the aforementioned *Hausmusik* being, of course, a category apart). This accounts for the restrained elegance of a Mozart piece using the *style hongrois* by comparison with, say, a Lisztian essay of the following century. Eighteenth-century musical convention required outside influences such as dances, or evocations of specific national styles, to be better assimilated into the prevailing style.

In the nineteenth century, the idea of a prevailing style was fast becoming outmoded. The musical languages of Weber and Schubert (to choose two early examples) were already moving far away from the standard musical "speech" of the eighteenth century, and when using the *style hongrois* they sought to intensify its dramatic effect rather than constrain it. Changing aesthetic and cultural preoccupations would also play their part in the way this style was heard and understood: there would be an increasing artistic interest in the strange, the terrible, and the exotic. The *style hongrois* ceased being merely a superficial reference to the musical style of Gypsy entertainers, and instead became an evocation of something much more immediate and powerful, with powerful extra-musical associations. In the eighteenth century, in other words, an *ongherese* was merely a topic;[16] the nineteenth-century *style hongrois* was a discrete musical language.

A convenient segue to the mature *style hongrois* is provided by Johann Nepomuk Hummel, himself a product of the eighteenth century, yet a lionized figure of the nineteenth. A student of Mozart and a celebrated virtuoso, his style centered on control and elegance rather than on thunderous effects and dramatic extremes, and his compositions—once popular, now all but forgotten—were fluent and charming, but perhaps more polite than successive generations of listeners would find challenging. He composed a set of pieces wholly in the *style hongrois,* the *Ballo Ongaresi* ("Hungarian Dances," ca. 1807). These were dedicated to the Princess Leopoldina of

Liechtenstein (born the Princess Esterházy, as he points out on the title page) and are clearly pieces with the taste and technique of an amateur in mind: they are brief, attractive, and relatively easy to play. They are not, however, elegant in the eighteenth-century sense. The opening piece, for example, is labelled *Ballo patetico,* and this and several others have a sort of heavy, *lassan*-like gait that at this time is emerging as a clear feature of the *style hongrois.* The second strophe of this dance, shown in example 16a, displays crying parallel thirds (later indispensable to the *style hongrois* as an imitation of eastern European vocal styles), triplet decorations, an arresting modal chord change from m. 12 to m. 13, the interval of an augmented second in m. 13, and a variety of ornaments. Example 16b shows the exaggerated syncopations and soloistic writing characteristic of a real Hungarian-Gypsy *friss* and 16c shows augmented seconds and chromatic inflections in the melody. Even though Hummel was Mozart's student, his brusque, heavily accented *style hongrois* is a far cry from a Mozartean *ongherese.* From this point forward, the *style hongrois* would become, in art music at least, an increasingly powerful and vivid language.

Contemporaneous with the blossoming of the *style hongrois* was the waning of the Turkish Style. It is certainly true that both styles coexisted for a time, often, as we have seen, in the same piece. While the earliest manifestations of the *style hongrois* reach back to the 1780s or slightly before, such works as Weber's Turkish opera *Abu Hassan* (1811) and the Turkish March from Beethoven's Ninth Symphony (finished 1824) testify to that style's relative longevity. I suspect that the real problem with the Turkish Style is that it had relatively little to express. The Turks had long since ceased to be any kind of threat, the shadow of the Siege was long forgotten, and the music itself could express variations on only one mood: a thumping, pounding march, or more properly 2/4 racket,

Example 16. Johann Nepomuk Hummel, *Balli Ongaresi* (ca. 1807).

16a. *Ballo* no. 1, mm. 9–16, parallel thirds, triplets, modal harmonic change, and ornaments.

16b. *Ballo* no. 2, mm. 5–8, *friss*-type writing.

16c. *Ballo* no. 4, mm. 5–8, brusque change of harmony, augmented seconds, affective chromatics.

suitable for either great celebration, fury, or mockery of the musical style and personality of the distant Turk. The novelty of such music must have worn off relatively quickly, such elevated examples as Mozart's notwithstanding, since it was best suited for light operatic entertainments and ephemeral instrumental works.

As the Turkish style was neither an elevated nor a multifaceted musical langauge, and the *style hongrois* was developing into precisely that, the newer exotic dialect's eclipse of the older was total. The *style hongrois* was capable of a wide range of emotion, from grief to abandon, utmost seriousness to frivolity, yet always with an accent and significance unattainable by more traditional musical language. What lent it this expressive power was less its country of origin than the people who disseminated it, because their extraordinary circumstances and situation in society lent both an aura of forbidden mystery and an allure to their music. It is to them that we now turn.

CHAPTER 4

Stereotypes: The Gypsies in Literature and Popular Culture

"GAILY LET US dispense with wealth, when we have it, let us accept poverty without worry, if it comes; let us keep above all our liberty, enjoy life all the same, and long live the Gypsy!"[1] This clarion call to inaction, from the final pages of George Sand's novel *La Dernière Aldini,* neatly summarizes the most favorable aspects of the Gypsy stereotype: freedom from material care, from covetousness, from emotional attachment to anything, and in a sense from caring at all. The Gypsies, with their transient existence and adventuring temperament, were seen as freedom made flesh. Part savage, part universal Other, part reminiscence of an idealized, strife-free past, they represented a whole range of ideas and emotions considered inappropriate, if not dangerous, to European society.

For the late twentieth century, of course, the relevance of this thoroughly fictional Gypsy is quite diminished. Today's surviving Gypsy stereotype, the residue from Romantic literature and Viennese operettas, is relatively benign. It is wholly unrelated to actual Gypsy problems such as the reawakening of ancient bigotries and resulting persecution in Germany and eastern Europe, for example, or the problems and challenges of the urban Rom in the United States. Like most stereotypes, in other words, its relationship to reality is almost nil. Compared to the nineteenth-century construct, our popular-culture image seems denatured, sanitized, and simplistic.

This nineteenth-century, popular-culture Gypsy was contradictory and multifaceted, the product of many different fears, concerns, and associations. The Romantic era had a fascination with the elemental and the forbidden, and would attribute great significance to an entire people living outside societal restrictions and mores. As the Romani culture was largely opaque to outsiders, it could be seen to reflect whatever society desired or dreaded. Not surprisingly, these imaginary Gypsies were found to have both fearsome and admirable, or at least enviable, qualities.

The nineteenth-century storybook Gypsies also had little relation to reality. In contrast to freedom, mystery, and magic, in the years preceding and during the Romantic movement the lives of most of Europe's Romani people were lived in abominable circumstances, unsuitable even for fiction. Occasionally fictional Gypsies served to inspire fear in *gadje* (non-Gypsies) but the stereotype's most powerful and immediate aspects could not approach the direness of reality. Accordingly, in fiction and poetry the Romani circumstances were lightly passed over in favor of the people's symbolic value as caution or temptation.

The Gypsies had begun to appear in German literature at about the same time as the emergence of the *style hongrois,* the first sighting being in an early work by the young Johann Wolfgang von Goethe. Goethe's play *Götz von Berlichingen* (1773) was one of the first salvos of the *Sturm und Drang* movement, in which young writers were beginning to abandon classical conventions of structure and situation. The presence of the Gypsies in his work reflects the increasing interest also shown by contemporary nonfiction sources, although his treatment of them is far more sympathetic. In this play, the forest Gypsies prove to be the last faithful protectors of the betrayed hero, the knight Götz. As the unjustly loathed and mistreated people struggle valorously to shield the noble but wronged and wounded knight, the poignancy and irony in Goethe's juxtaposition is inescapable.

Ludwig Achim von Arnim's *Isabella von Ägypten* (1812) plays on another aspect of the same phenomenon, and it testifies to what editor Alfred Schier called "[Arnim's] sympathy for the Gypsies . . . the homelessness, the prophecy, the unluckiness and the tragedy of an entire people."[2] The tale centers on Isabella, the daughter of Prince Michael of Egypt and the last trace of his noble Gypsy lineage, who is astray in Europe with her people. Arnim manages to incorporate here just a hint of one of the most damaging Gypsy stereotypes: a curse, the eternal punishment for an ancient crime, which amounts to tainted blood and an inheritance of guilt passed down through generations of Gypsies. Isabella is aware of her circumstances:

> She also knew the old crime of her people, that they would not give the Holy Mother Mary shelter on her flight to Egypt when she entered with her beatific son in the strong rain; then [the child] lifted his hand in a circle, and over them stood a rainbow, that no drop could fall on them. "Has our guilt not yet been expiated!" sighed Bella.[3]

The idea of an ancient curse on the Gypsies recurs in the literature, incidentally, and is recounted in different form by Clemens Brentano, Arnim's brother-in-law, as an introduction to his poem based on the same story, *Die Romanzen vom Rosenkranz* (written during the early nineteenth century).[4] This tale, too byzantine and unpalatable to summarize, is more damaging in that, from the starting point of a union between a Crusader and a Gypsy girl, it fuels the most virulent anti-Gypsy accusations: theft, violence, attempted murder, a curse from the Virgin Mary, incest, and the seemingly free exchange of children and wives. It is a deplorable mixture of German race-consciousness, in which the guilt for Gypsy crimes is passed on to succeeding generations, and hand-wringing Christian piety, as character after character wreaks evil and only afterward enters the cloister, while their children continue to pour out the wrath of the curse on themselves and future generations.

All this forms an obvious parallel to the supposed curse on the Jews resulting from their refusal to acknowledge Jesus as Messiah, or more specifically the legend of Ahashuerus, the Wandering Jew.[5] The anti-Gypsy legend does not have even a slight biblical connection or excuse; Gypsies are not mentioned there. There was, simply, a cultural need for a religious curse that would afford a sanction to mistreat outsiders. Such mistreatment could thus be lent a kind of divine justification. Arnim, in contrast to Brentano, does not pursue this putative ancient guilt past its value as a narrative premise; excepting the hanging of Isabella's father following an accusation of chicken theft, his treatment of the Gypsies is relatively gentle. Isabella herself is adored by her people and is clearly an idealized type:

> Bella belonged to a species of migrant bird, that despite all the tender care and love of man, if it hears the voices of its brothers in the air, cannot resist. . . . Her longing, her melancholy inundated her boundlessly; she could not stay and did not know why.[6]

She knew only the grandeur of poverty which owns
everything because it can disdain everything.[7]

We are reminded of the introductory quotation from George
Sand: poverty was seen as the Gypsy's conscious choice and
badge of honor, with a spirit as free as the zephyr.

Even at this early stage of German *Zigeunerromantik,* Isabella is not a wholly original character. A fairylike, bewitching Gypsy girl is the central figure in a seventeenth-century
Spanish work, Miguel de Cervantes' *La Gitanilla* (The Little
Gypsy Girl). This work, one of the author's *Novellas Exem-
plares* of 1613, tells a simple story: the most eye-catching of a
group of Spanish Gypsies is a sparkling girl called Preciosa,
who so capitvates the young son of a nobleman that he
abandons everything to join her Gypsy band, taking the name
Andrés so as to marry her. As the drama reaches its climax,
however, she is revealed by her Gypsy "grandmother" to be
no Gypsy at all, but a young woman of noble blood who
was raised by the Gypsies since infancy. Thus, the ensuing
marriage is between two nobles, signifying a happy ending.

La Gitanilla, which Arnim certainly knew,[8] is a story
particularly accommodating to a race-conscious sensibility.
Initially, Cervantes' character is charmingly exotic, but once
the reader falls in love with her, her charm is seen to be the
result of noble blood, which is free of race admixture or
Gypsy criminality. This work, while not as idealized as
Arnim's *Isabella,* still treats the Gypsy stereotype (such as it
existed in 1613) relatively gently.[9] Nonetheless, it does con-
tain the following:

> Gipsies seem to have been born into the world for the
> sole purpose of being thieves: they are born of thieving
> parents, they are brought up with thieves, they study in
> order to be thieves, and they end up as past masters in
> the art of thieving. Thieving and the taste for thieving

are inseparable from their existence, and they never abandon them till they reach the grave.[10]

> When these ceremonies were over, an old gipsy took Preciosa by the hand, and standing in front of Andrés he said: "This girl, who is the cream of all the most beautiful gipsy girls in Spain that we know, we give to you, as wife, or as mistress; because in this matter you can do whatever you best please, for our free and easy life is not subject to finicky ceremonial. Examine her well, and see if she pleases you, or if you see in her anything which you don't like, and if you do see anything, choose from among these girls here the one you like best, for we will give you whichever one you choose."[11]

Aside from unlimited freedom (which is, at least in comparison with violence and incest, morally neutral), the associations of theft and easy virtue are among those that recurred in "nonfictional" Gypsy discussions in ever more virulent form. Further, they could easily be interpreted as direct results of freedom in excess. Liberation from societal constraints and material considerations would imply not only disdaining property, as with Arnim's Isabella, but also disdaining others' rights of ownership of it, which implies theft. Aloof contempt for the manners and morals of society could only lead to one thing: sexual promiscuity, and it is to this that Cervantes' old Gypsy alludes despite the fact that it does not affect the perfect and untouchable Preciosa. *(La Gitanilla* would reappear as *Preciosa,* Pius Alexander Wolff's German adaptation, for which Carl Maria von Weber wrote music. This will be discussed in the section devoted to that composer.) Even with the presence of theft and easy morals, though, Cervantes' Gypsies still get passably gentle treatment.

Contrary to what we will see in putative nonfiction, the

fictional treatment of the Gypsies in Great Britain also tended to be relatively humane. Sir Walter Scott's *Guy Mannering* (1815) was almost dangerously colorful in referring to the Gypsies' "wild features, dark eyes, and swarthy faces" in its famous Gypsy curse episode. To set the stage, the author offers an account of the Gypsies in Scotland, which includes the following uncomplimentary passage:

> They lost . . . the national character of the Egyptians, and became a mingled race, having all the idleness and predatory habits of their eastern ancestors, with a ferocity that they probably borrowed from the men of the north who joined their society.[12]

This sentiment notwithstanding, the Gypsies in this novel respond at worst only to blatant mistreatment. Indeed, Scott takes pains to show one old Gypsy woman as an affectionate lookout for a lord's adventurous young son. Despite a powerful curse she wishes on the lord who banishes her and her people from his land, it is her dying words that save young Harry Bertram, the lord's son, from unjust punishment in later years. The Gypsies here are vivid, picturesque, but more unfathomable than profoundly troubling.

Gentler still are the poems of Matthew Arnold, who focused on, among other qualities, the profound grief associated with the Gypies:

> Who taught this pleading to unpractised eyes?
> Who hid such import in an infant's gloom?
> Who lent thee, child, this meditative guise?
> Who mass'd, round that slight brow, these clouds of
>   doom? . . .
>
> Glooms that go deep as thine I have not known:
> Moods of fantastic sadness, nothing worth.
> Thy sorrow and thy calmness are thine own:
> Glooms that enhance and glorify this earth.
>
> What mood wears like complexion to thy woe? . . .

Some exile's, mindful of how the past was glad?
Some angel's, in an alien planet born?[13]

More idealized, yet is *The Scholar-Gypsy* (1853), Arnold's
meditation on an English legend involving an Oxford scholar
who meets and joins a Gypsy band. He goes to learn their
secret arts, their supposed knowledge of the workings of the
human mind and so forth, abandoning his previous life and
scholarly aspirations. But the characterization of the Gypsies
is gentle and detached; again, they are merely elusive, dark,
and mysterious.

This illustrates one of the guiding principles in the literary
use of Gypsies: the exaggeration of the most relevant part of
the stereotype. If the author needs loneliness and gloom, this
is what the Gypsies represent; if a threatening criminal class
is called for, particularly where theft is concerned, the Gypsies can always serve; if one simply needs a group of wanderers, the Gypsies come immediately to mind. They also do
yeoman's duty as the personification of sexual infidelity,
particularly in cases where circumstances have led one's characters into temptation.

This latter is particularly well illustrated in a work by
Alexander Pushkin. His play *The Gypsies* (1824; later an opera
by Rakhmaninov called *Aleko),* as a study of the protagonist
Aleko's alienation, stresses both the traditional Gypsy allure
and treachery. Aleko, tired and despondent, forsakes the
world and decides to follow the Gypsies, in the meantime
falling in love with a beautiful Gypsy girl. Similar to Mérimée's *Carmen* (1847; later an opera by Bizet[14]), disaster results:
a year later, Aleko's Gypsy has betrayed him, he kills both
her and her lover, and her old father offers a sad and resigned
postscript about his own betrayal by the girl's mother. The
traditional Gypsy associations of wandering, irresistible attraction, and betrayal thus underscore the Wertherian depths

of the romantic antihero: while the Gypsies initially represent for Aleko a new family of similarly mistreated humanity, he is betrayed even by one of them.

One of the most famous literary uses of the Gypsies is Victor Hugo's *Notre Dame de Paris* (1840). Hugo's Gypsies are malevolent stealers of babies, and in general provoke revulsion. Esmerelda, a beautiful and clever Gypsy girl, turns out (as with Cervantes' Preciosa) to be no Gypsy at all; she had been stolen by them from her poor mother, who had been forced into a fallen condition by cruel circumstances. Indeed, the Gypsies' presence in the story seems necessary only to provide occasional gruesome color and to have committed this villainy before the story actually begins.

But this example touches on another far-reaching Gypsy association. Baby snatching such as this is one of the oldest and most enduring of all accusations. It has a strong racial aspect, as it was assumed that the dark-skinned Gypsies coveted white-skinned European children and stole them whenever possible. It is therefore notable that the aforementioned Gypsy in Scott's *Guy Mannering* loves the lord's child Bertram, follows him, and gives him sweets, but does not steal him. Despite the idea's persistence, of course, this crime has never been a documented practice among Gypsies. The response of a fearful public to even the suggestion of it may well be imagined, however, and it was a typical charge for the Rom to face.

Even with their unwholesome elements, as reflections of the popular culture these literary treatments are relatively benign by comparison with ostensibly nonfiction sources, which offer a frankly demonized picture of the Gypsies. Encyclopedia articles, for example, seem to be lacking anything approaching the sort of objectivity we might hope to see in twentieth-century reference sources and can resemble mere collections of accusations. Travelogues, too, tended to emphasize the lurid and frightening; although in none of them did I encounter a description of any actual threatening or unpleasant encounters with Gypsies, the authors' descriptions often reflected the worst of contemporary biases.

We have already encountered fears of the Gypsies as suspected spies of the Turk, both before the Siege of Vienna and some seventy years after it. The Gypsies initially appeared in western Europe in the early fifteenth century,[15] and the connection with the suspect Turkish East dogged them for centuries. The initial fear seems to be no more than fear of the unknown: the Gypsies were dark, they were migratory (although peaceably so), they kept quite separate as a people— their alien character and lifestyle were simply assumed to be threatening. In a Europe where people and their native land were to a certain extent conceptually inseparable, a wandering people, distinct in appearance and behavior, was immediate cause for suspicion and hatred.

In fact, it was the Gypsies' wandering life that most mystified Europeans. It became so fixed in the European mind that the settled Gypsies, of whom there were substantial numbers, were still thought of as foreign, different, and somehow impermanent. One German reference work from the early 1820s defined Gypsies simply as "wandering people in Europe and Asia, of unknown origin; in Hungary, Galicia and the Bukowine they are also called *New Hungarians,* 60,000 heads strong."[16] The Austrian National Encyclopedia of 1837 expands on the wandering idea, providing a bit more detail:

> These wanderers are treated everywhere with scorn
> and contempt. . . . They do not like to settle down;
> most of them follow their overpowering partiality to the
> wandering life, and roam with their tents through the
> land, where they prefer to seek out unbeaten paths and
> gloomy mountain ravines. . . . The wandering, or so-
> called Egyptian beggar Gypsies, unfamiliar with all the

benefits of civilization, and hampered by their inherited condemnation from grasping the opportunities for the bettering of their fate which present themselves, these people lead a most miserable life. Without having a permanent residence, they wander, summer and winter, from one place to another.[17]

A settled Europe had no easy explanation for such a lifestyle. In addition to the legendary religious curse (one aspect, certainly, of the "inherited condemnation"), there began to evolve a list of antisocial behaviors imputed to the Gypsies and heinous offenses of which they were felt to be guilty. These, of course, could then be interpreted as proof of the curse's justification. From the earliest times, as we saw in Cervantes, come the strongest and the most common accusations: theft and robbery.

These fears were certainly still present at the time of the Siege. We already saw Edward Brown's comments from 1673 on the "stout" and "bold" Hungarian Gypsies, some of whom had "been noted robbers." More than a century later William Macmichael, also an Englishman, echoed this with his observation that "the pilfering and roguish dispositions observable among them in England, characterize them also in Moldavia,"[18] and their compatriot the Reverend Robert Walsh alludes to the Gypsies' presumed dishonesty by expressing surprise when a young female travelling companion of his, who was holding her baby, turned out to be a Gypsy yet had somehow neglected to rob him. Their carriage stops at a series of low huts, and he comments:

> These I found were inhabited by a race of settled Bohemians, somewhat reclaimed from their wandering life; and here my companion and her child stopped and got out. I had been travelling for the first time in my life with a young Gipsey [*sic*]; and it struck me that she might have exercised her professional talents on what-

ever she could lay her hand: but she was an honest and a
proper girl, and seemed a very kind mother to her little
child. Before I set forward again, she came, with some
of her tribe, to thank and take leave of me.[19]

The Reverend Robert Walsh, as we will shortly see, did not
let this pleasant experience interfere with an opportunity to
recount the most extreme Gypsy stereotypes.

German sources tended to be far harsher on the issue of
robbery and theft. An encyclopedia article from 1841 states,

> The appearance of the men is mostly repulsive, and
> in their features is expressed a certain shyness as well as
> a love for indolence and freedom, which, with propen-
> sity to cheating and thievery, is above all inherent in
> their character. They do not possess courage and ven-
> ture even nighttime burglary only very rarely, and then
> only when they can do it safely; on the other hand, they
> display much cunning and ingenuity in their undertak-
> ings.[20]

An earlier reference work minces even fewer words, saying,

> They were at the very least liars, who try to get by
> with all kinds of falsehoods about their own circum-
> stances. . . . They were insolent beggars, who got
> through craft or force what they could not get through
> goodness of heart; thus they were well set up, through
> all kinds of schemes and cheating, to rob people of their
> money.[21]

Insufficient religiosity was one predictable complement of
this battery of antisocial behaviors. After all, where moral
standards were imagined to be lacking, could a proper
grounding be in evidence? One of the most frustrating things
a native populace noticed about the Gypsies was that they
had no apparent religion of their own that believers could
then, in good conscience, despise (as was the case, for example, with Moslems or Jews). The Gypsies were observed to

practice the religion of the land, although this usually was not in and of itself enough to earn societal goodwill. This testimony dates from 1841:

> Their religious practices conform for the most part to those that prevail in the country in which they stay; and as they are Mohammedans in Turkey, so they are out-wardly Christians in Siebenbürgen, Hungary and Spain, but without caring anything about the conception of study of spiritual things. Not infrequently, it happens that they have their children baptized repeatedly in various places, in order to receive gifts from godparents several times.[22]

This discussion is heartwarming in its implication that most or all members of any religious group might have, in fact, a developed "conception of study of spiritual things." It is in issues like this that such criticisms serve as excuses for sheer bigotry. Nowhere in this clearer than in the account of Mr. Walsh. Immediately following his bemused surprise at the benevolence of his encounter with the young Gypsy mother, he launches into a long discussion of the Gypsies and their habits, a discussion that rivals the worst of the German sources in pure venom. Here is the segment dealing with the Gypsies' practice of Christianity (and we must remember that Walsh was a seminarian):

> They acknowledge no particular religion as their own, but generally confess the Greek rites, of which they have but a crude and debased conception. They baptize their children; but it is generally done by them-selves in a public-house, with a profaine [*sic*] mixture of ribaldry and folly. They have no notion of a resurrec-tion, independent of the same body being again brought to life before it decays, which they say is impossible. One of their children died at school in this place, and the parents requested he might be buried with his school-fellows. On being asked if they expected to meet

him in a future state, they said they knew he could never
live again; and showing a skinned horse, asked whether
it was possible that could be ever restored to life.[23]

Note, here, the implied equation of one of their own
children's souls with that of a dead horse. This anecdote is
reminiscent of the legendary curse on the Gypsy people in
that it underscores their supposed godlessness, which in any
group has historically meant the relative guiltlessness of those
who persecuted them. Not only were the Gypsies understood
to be at odds in every respect with the general code of
behavior, but in apparently denying the resurrection of the
soul after death they were really denying the divine part of
humankind. If this were an accurate indication of the state of
their souls, then their debased condition in society required
neither explanation nor concern. Even Heinrich Grellmann,
one of the first scholarly students of the Gypsies (whose first
study appeared in 1760) acknowledged feeling "an evident
repugnancy, like a biologist dissecting some nauseating,
crawling thing in the interests of science." More to the point
was the remark of a contemporary of his, a Lithuanian
minister named Zippel: "Gypsies in a well-ordered state in
the present day are like vermin on an animal's body."[24]

An infestation of vermin is precisely what was implied in
discussions of the Gypsies' physical hygiene. Horror tales
describing their wagons and dwellings inspired the imagination, and stories of utter befoulment surrounded the Gypsy
tribes despite traditional Gypsy customs of cleanliness, ritual
purity, and so forth. While occasionally a more honest ob-
server commented that the Gypsy wagons were, if small and
cramped, quite clean inside, this perspective was rarely voiced
in comparison with the nightmarish accounts of bestial living
conditions and general degradation.

Again, the reference sources and travelogues bear ample
witness to this view. On the moderate side of the discussion

is this remark, from the mid-eighteenth century: "The Gypsies were of swarthy coloring, and not very clean in their clothing or in the rest of their behaviors. They claimed to be Christians and purported to come from Little Egypt."[25] Some decades later, the Austrian National Encyclopedia had the following to say:

> In the summer they usually live in tents, in the winter in miserable earthen huts. It is easy to imagine how disgusting the inside of such a Gypsy hut appears. The air and sunlight can scarcely find an entrance. The entire inner space consists of one communal area, in the middle of which a fire burns, which serves simultaneously to warm themselves and to prepare their meals.[26]

Practices of child rearing and eating habits also had great shock value:

> The children are seldom provided with clothing before their tenth year. This is true primarily for the wandering Gypsies. . . . Every kind of meat is good to them, and dogs, cats, rats, mice, and even fallen livestock are consumed by them. What is more, in the previous century in Hungary, Gypsies were even accused of having eaten human flesh and were severely punished for that reason, although no one was able to prove it.[27]

But it is again Walsh who provides the most vivid description:

> When inclined to a settled life, several families herd together, with pigs and other animals, in a small enclosure, which is rendered exceedingly offensive by their total disregard of cleanliness.
>
> They are in temper irascible, even to frenzy, and live in a state of constant discord with each other, which is greatly increased by a propensity to intoxication. Notwithstanding their debased and despised situation in society, they are proud and consequential, exceedingly loquacious and vainglorious, with no regard to truth.

. . . Notwithstanding their general depravity, there are
grades of infamy, and many are so vile that they are
rejected by the rest; of these some are made execution-
ers, who set about the task with delight, prepare extraordinary instruments of torture, and take a savage
pleasure in telling the victim the punishment he is to
undergo, and the pain he is to suffer. . . . They are also
employed as scullions, and contribute to increase that
dirt and disorder for which a Wallachian kitchen in
notorious.[28]

Along with the Gypsies' wandering, their mysterious and
suspect past, their debased Christianity, accusations of theft
and robbery, and the supposed predisposition to living in
filth, it should not be surprising to find suspicion of their
sexual mores included in the same picture. This was generally
represented in a much more loathesome way than the mere
allure and fickleness of the Gypsies of literature. Although
later research has suggested that in most families rituals of
marriage and cleanliness kept the women quite separate from
the native populace, suggestions of easy virtue and of the
seductive, exotic, and ultimately faithless Gypsy lover
emerged—more from the European subconscious, one is
tempted to add, than from the Gypsies themselves. One
German source, for example, describes the women as "often
of a very charming appearance in their younger years, yet are
also, as a rule, wanton and cunning paramours."[29] Apparent,
here, is the stereotype that gave rise to Pushkin's unfaithful
Gypsy girl, and Mérimée's Carmen. Related to this is the
assumption that the marriage vows ostensibly held sacred in
Christian society were of but scant importance to the Gypsies. The example from Cervantes is one manifestation of
this stereotype; the German source continues: "Marriages
happen with such little ceremony that marital fidelity is kept
with little strictness.[30] Mr. Walsh had obviously heard the
same stories:

> They form connexions before they are of marriage-
> able years, and change them as inclination leads; and
> mothers are frequently surrounded by a number of
> children of different fathers, who, to a certain age, run
> about naked even in the severest weather.[31]

The scholar David Mayall relates the libidinous aspect of the Gypsy stereotype to the wandering itself, summarizing both the following way: "[The Gypsies] were free-living and free-loving, with a sexual appetite matched only by their wanderlust, itself a product of the possession of black blood, or *kalo ratt*. The wild nomadic spirit was transmitted by birth and could not be controlled or denied."[32] Notice the gradual evolution: the ideas of aimless wandering and flight gradually become freedom, the lure of the road, wanderlust, and adventure. Clearly, literature and Romanticism are playing their part here, as successive European cultural environments inform the concepts of the Gypsies and their place in society.

The emotional makeup of the Gypsies is integral to the stereotype. Their *kalo ratt* disposed them, it was thought, to wild celebration and exultation; their talent for musical expression and entertainment was another manifestation of this same propensity. They were also supposedly subject to a profound, almost animal melancholy, the natural wages of their ancient curse, their wandering, and their persecution. Mercurial, almost childlike changes between these primitive emotional states reinforced two aspects of their reputation: first, people whose emotional responses to life were pure, genuine, and unencumbered by propriety, and second, beings so simplistic and unaffected as to be barely human.

Wild, extraordinary joy is mentioned in none of the earlier nonfiction sources, and it seems to result from interpreting the Gypsies' successive banishments and flight as freedom and adventuring and is therefore a product of the European imagination. Joyful demeanor during their musical performances could easily be interpreted as the expression of their innermost feelings, although as appropriate to the situation it is no more than one would expect of any commercial entertainer. This is a very different issue from their imputed ethnic melancholy, which almost all sources mention. To the popular psychology, it suited their dark skin color and the tales of divine punishment resulting in ceaseless flight and eternal exile. But the reality was worse than mere flight and exile; in the German and central European lands the Gypsies suffered abominable persecution and mistreatment in the eighteenth and nineteenth centuries. It is more than probable that a very real depression and melancholy did characterize the Rom at this time and that it could easily be read in the faces of those facing such circumstances on a daily basis.

In eighteenth-century, Hapsburg-ruled Hungary, the Gypsies had been publically designated a scourge and were openly pursued and tormented with the intent to rid the land of them. For example, one particularly draconian order of Charles VI dates from 1726 and stipulated the following punishments for Gypsies discovered in the country: adult males were to be killed on the spot, and women and children were to have their ears cut off and be whipped all the way to the border.[33] In 1782, forty or so Gypsies were accused of roasting and eating several dozen Hungarian peasants, for which they were broken on the wheel and afterwards cut into pieces. Although these charges remained unproven, and Emperor Joseph II later declared them to be utterly groundless, this episode resonated in the German imagination. It is widely recounted in later sources dealing with the Gypsies (as we saw above), with the occasional addition of implied vampirism, but the victims' innocence was only grudgingly acknowledged.[34] In any case, the sport of Gypsy hunting continued into the next century: one Baron von Lenchen put his trophies, the heads of a Gypsy woman and her child, on public display in 1826, while in 1835 a Rheinland aristocrat recorded "a Gypsy woman and her suckling babe" on his list of kills.[35]

This behavior was legally and culturally sanctioned. The entry for *Zigeuner* in an encyclopedia of 1749 states openly that "certainly Gypsies have been godless, evil people for all time, and are persecuted for good reason."[36] Later in the same article, we find the following:

> Now since this Gypsy-folk is in the habit of causing much mischief, as it is now reported, thus it is certainly a fair and just punishment for this people that they are searched out with force of arms in all places (be it in cities, boroughs, villages, bushes, and woods) and expelled out of the country by force, as it is ordered almost everywhere in Germany; it is permitted to shoot and kill them on the spot for perceived resistance, and to arrest and inflict bodily and capital punishment upon them without any mercy or investigation, and without any further process, simply and solely on account of their forbidden moral conduct and manifest insubordination; however, the women and children [are] condemned for life in penitentiaries and workhouses.[37]

Note how far this reality is from allure, mystery, and the freedom of life on the road. A melancholy demeanor and low morale resulting from this unimaginable abuse would seem to be an appropriate response and did soon become part of the cultural stereotype. The Austrian National Encyclopedia of 1837 offers the following description:

> On the brow of a Gypsy, surrounded by long, black hair, one can usually read deep melancholy; the black eyes look gloomily out from under dark eyelashes, and there is no feature in the countenance that does not indicate sadness and gloomy brooding. Not their children, not their wives arouse their compassion; the entire weight of the sad fate of this outcast people seems to

press upon their souls, and their aspect is suited to inspire the deepest sympathy. These wanderers are treated everywhere with scorn and contempt, and even the rough Wallachians (full of physical and moral defects) look down on the Gypsies with disdain.[38]

In the Rumanian lands, Moldavia and Wallachia, the brutal reality was that until the last quarter of the nineteenth century the Gypsies were legal slaves. A French journalist, Félix Colson, visited the Balkans in 1839 and kept a diary in which he described the circumstances of this slave class. The household Gypsies of his host (a Rumanian aristocrat) had privileged status and relatively light duties, although for the females these duties included sexually servicing master and guests. Rather than pride in their elevated position, the slaves' visible response was precisely what we might expect it to be; in Colson's words, "misery is so clearly painted on the faces of these slaves that, if you happened to glance at one, you'd lose your appetite."[39]

Entirely aside from their real situation, and apart from their overwhelmingly poisonous reputation, negative character traits did not form the whole stereotype. In more objective discussions, certain noncriminal areas of expertise were granted to the Gypsies, the foremost and most widely acknowledged being music. For example, following a discussion of their unfortunate circumstances, the Austrian National Encyclopedia points out,

> Yet [the Gypsy] is full of natural capabilities, a jack-of-all-trades, who tries everything, possesses talents and gifts for everything. . . . Now, they are the most excellent musicians in Hungary, and unsurpassable in Hungarian performance. . . . They are masters not only in the making and handling of instruments, but also [they are] even imaginative composers and poets, even if they never write down a note, or ever even know a note.[40]

Walsh was in agreement; after his unsurpassably slanderous account of the Gypsies, he closes with these surprisingly positive comments on their musical ability:

> They have naturally very acute and delicate perceptions of sounds, and hence they are greatly disposed to and delighted with music: this talent is much cultivated; and they form usually the musicians of these countries, particularly on wind instruments. I have often heard them play, and always with pleasure.[41]

And Johann Georg Kohl, travelling in Hungary around 1840, left this short and vivid description of a Gypsy performance that captures the entire ambience:

> But the gypsies [play] the true national compositions of Hungary, which breathe a peculiar spirit, and are distinguished by certain original turns and phrases, which I never remember to have heard anywhere else. . . . I could easily understand the partiality manifested by the people generally for this music, for there is something in its character so wild and impassioned—it has tones of such deep melancholy, such heart-piercing grief, and wild despair, that one is unvoluntarily carried away by it; and although, on the whole, the performance of the gypsies is rude and wild, many of them manifest so much of musical inspiration, as may well make amends for their deficiencies in scientific culture.[42]

Perhaps the most thorough representation of the Gypsy stereotype, musical and otherwise, is found in *Des Bohémiens et de leur musique en Hongrie,* first published in 1859, by Franz Liszt. Admittedly, it stresses the positive aspects of the stereotype: musical ability, freedom, special relationship to nature, and so forth. As this is a relatively late source, and one that tells us more about its author(s) than about its subject, we will examine it in more detail later: the musical aspects in chapter 5, and extramusical matters in chapter 8.

One fascinating result of the Gypsies' fame and reputation in the musical and entertainment spheres was that the word *Gypsy* took on a kind of double meaning. The art historian Marilyn Brown quotes a theater review by Théophile Gautier from 1843 to underscore this point; in France, the word *Bohémien,* which had signified "Gypsy" from the Gypsies' first appearance in that country (because they came from the east, where Bohemia lay), took on a different meaning that had no ethnic significance whatever, but rather suggested a kind of lifestyle. In explaining the difference between the actual Rom and the emerging "Bohemian" artist, Gautier said:

> These children [the Rom] of la bohème have their hierarchy, their religion, their rites; their origin is lost in the night of time; their migrations inspire poetry. . . . There is also another species of bohemian no less charming and poetic; it consists of foolish youth which lives somewhat haphazardly from day to day by its intelligence: painters, musicians, actors, poets, journalists, who love pleasure more than money and who prefer laziness and liberty to everything, even glory; an amiable race full of ease and good instincts . . . which forgets daily bread for evening conversation. . . . We have all been more or less members of that *bohème:* a happy time when we imagined we had debts . . . when we got drunk on our youth while drinking a glass of water. . . . Along with the gitanos of Spain, the gypsies of Scotland, the *zigueners* [*sic*] of Germany, here are the only bohemians that we recognize.[43]

Brown quotes Charles Dickens's *Household Words* (1851) to the same effect, and concludes: "The word 'bohemian' was filled with multiple significations, and in the works of numerous artists the visual sign of gypsies and related wanderers became rich in potential metaphor."[44] This is illustrated by the many idealized artistic representations that form the subject of Brown's study, which documents the romanticized side of the Gypsy-artist stereotype in the visual art of the nineteenth century. The evolution of meaning is a fascinating one: the stereotyped "bohemian" lifestyle first related to the Gypsy people itself, then became associated with their own musical talent, and finally was understood to apply to any musician or entertainer living in casual circumstances. These sorts of circumstances, of course, are still characterized by the word *bohemian* today.

But the relationship goes deeper. One of the Gypsy characteristics that most infuriated Europeans was their defiant adherence to their own preferences in terms of lifestyle and mores. The most horrible persecutions could not be seen to convince them to mend their ways, so there was a clear implication that they held their manner of living to be superior to that of their neighbors. Of course, this ties in with freedom and independence, and the idea of following one's own course in the face of the strongest possible opposition. Formidable opposition, unfriendly circumstances, and a marginalized existence are and have always been the daily bread of musicians, artists, poets, and playwrights, so the kinship can be understood in that context also. It was the Gypsies' apparent steadfastness that held greatest significance for the musicians and artists who considered themselves their spiritual cousins.

Apart from the musical attractiveness of the *style hongrois,* the extramusical associations made it even more effective for a composer to use. The Romantic situation of the musician, mistreated and ignored but holding to his own course and answering only to the inner fire of inspiration, could be expressed by musical reference to an entire ethnic group in the same predicament. As we have seen, however, the Gypsy stereotype was multifaceted; in addition to a talented musician, "Gypsy" meant endless wandering, societal contempt and abuse, freedom with all its positive and negative implications, and both metahuman despair and a savage joy. The *style hongrois* suggested, therefore, extremes of emotion inaccessible to normal people, attainable only to the elemental tribe who lived in the wild and travelled with the wind and rain. In the Romantic era, these were also accessible to those few chosen by Art: composers, poets, writers, and playwrights.

As the *style hongrois* matured, a more complex, two-tiered significance began to evolve. From the beginning of the nineteenth century onward, Gypsies were increasingly popular as cafe entertainers and providers of light music, as might befit a musical caste. On one level, particularly in *Hausmusik,* the music would keep these associations: light, attractive, exotic, and colorful. We have also seen, however, that one part of the complex Gypsy stereotype involved lying and cheating. There arose a suggestion of dissembling, of masking true feelings, in certain uses of the *style hongrois:* rejoicing in the face of sadness and inner rage, maintaining bravery and haughtiness in the face of exile and mistreatment, glorifying the life of the road while in reality flying before the forces of damnation and punishment. These subtler meanings are most clearly illustrated in the music of Weber and Schubert, who perceived and exploited them, but they were in fact implicit in the contradictions, complexities, and mysteries of the stereotyped Romantic Gypsy.

CHAPTER 5

A Lexicon for the Style Hongrois

The pleasure of transferring to our instrument the
. . . reveries, effusions and exaltations of this wild
muse seemed to become more and more seductive
. . . to include the quintessence of their most remark-
able qualities, and form a compendium of their most
striking beauties.
Such a compendium . . . might fairly be regarded as
a national Epic—Bohemian Epic—and the strange
tongue in which its strains would be delivered would
be no stranger than everything else done by the
people from whom it emanated.

—Franz Liszt, *The Gipsy in Music*

THE INDIVIDUAL GESTURES of the emergent and maturing
style hongrois fall into several broad categories. One easily
identifiable group consists of imitations of the instruments
most commonly used by the Gypsies, and the characteristic
ways in which these instruments were played. A second

group is made up of rhythmic figures that became associated with the Gypsies' performances, these being both declamatory rhythms deriving from the Hungarian language and common ornamental and dance rhythms. A third group consists of melodic gestures, including both actual melodic figures typical of Hungarian-Gypsy music and the more general emphasis of specific, highly colored intervals. The fourth major group of gestures associated with the *style hongrois* is harmonic; although harder to codify in specific terms, these color the entire musical environment and are among the most compelling aspects of the language.

In connection with this "lexicon" we will make extensive acquaintance with the musical passages and discussions from Liszt's *The Gipsy in Music.* His colorful descriptions of the Gypsies' playing are valuable for a variety of reasons. They illustrate the fact that one of the greatest composers in this style identified as characteristic and noteworthy many of the same aspects we do today, which after almost a century and a half validates our comprehension of the style. As his book was not intended for specialists, he describes this music with the general reader of his time in mind, and in doing so puts into words how he thought this language ought to be heard and understood. Since the *style hongrois* is no longer an actively "spoken" language, that aspect of his book is of inestimable value to the late twentieth century.

One caveat: identifying individual components of the *style hongrois* with either the source music or instrumental gesture of origin is a somewhat inexact process, one made even more inexact by the peripatetic lifestyle of the Gypsies themselves. As they came west from Hungary, almost all their musical raw materials were Hungarian. Nonetheless, there can be discerned an occasional faintly Russian tint, or a Rumanian inflection, or an element from further east. This is only to be expected; as musicians in primarily an oral tradition the

Gypsies were free to assimilate whatever they heard into their own performance style, and they would certainly have been exposed to other Eastern musics from time to time. This much is clear: once a particular example or gesture made it to Vienna as part of the *style hongrois,* it would then be used or reinterpreted by the Viennese composers and be associated with the Hungarian Gypsies who brought it, rather than with whatever its actual district of origin.

By way of introduction, let us examine one singular passage that offers a clear illustration of the transition from actual Gypsy performance to *style hongrois* evocation. Rather than a single gesture, this encompasses a series of gestures in variation form, transcribed literally. Liszt states:

> The true Bohemian masters are those who, having syncopated their theme so as to give it a slight swinging effect, restore it to the normal measure as if preparing to lead a dance; after which it appears, as it were, casting sparks in every direction by clusters of small shakes.[1]

Liszt had originally intended this book to be an introduction to his Hungarian Rhapsodies, and the connection between the two works is nowhere clearer than here. This exact sequence appears in Liszt's arrangement of the fourteenth Hungarian Rhapsody, the *Hungarian Fantasia* for piano and orchestra, in the passage labeled "Allegretto alla Zingarese" (see example 17). This flirtatious theme is given first in a swung rhythm (17a), then straight (17b), then (after a short contrasting interlude) in a trill variation (17c), following the description precisely. As a general rule, however, it is individual gestures that are imitated and combined in *style hongrois* works, not entire minidiscourses or chains of variations.

Instruments and Instrumental Styles.   Unquestionably, the instrument most closely associated with Gypsies and the *style hongrois* is the fiddle. The most famous Gypsy bandleaders,

Example 17. Liszt, *Hungarian Fantasia* for piano and orchestra, *Allegretto alla Zingarese* section.

17a. Mm. 133–36.

17b. Mm. 141–44.

17c. Mm. 168–70.

Panna Czinka and János Bihari, were fiddlers, and it is this instrument (the Gypsies' documented reputation for wind music notwithstanding) that is most often associated with rhapsodic Gypsy performances. Liszt's descriptions always presuppose that the Gypsy band's fiddler is in a position of primacy, and the balance of Schubert's *style hongrois* melodies, such as many of those in his *Divertissement à l'Hongroise* (D. 818), have a decidedly violinistic cast.

There are several fiddle techniques that are specifically associated with Hungarian-Gypsy playing. Small, jangling ornaments and grace notes constitute one category: these might be a holdover from the Turkish Style, but regardless of origin they are ubiquitous. Nonmelodic, scratching extremes of range are also common, almost as if the composer were poking fun at a relatively unrefined Gypsy approach to fiddle playing in general. (This is reminiscent of the third movement from Haydn's String Quartet, op. 20/4, in which the appellation *Minuetto alla Zingarese* seems to mean nothing more than *pesante;* other than rude accents on every beat the movement does not reflect the *style hongrois* at all.) One particularly interesting example suggests double stops alternating with much lower single notes; it hints at a kind of rude scraping, or even tuning up. Example 18 gives two instances of this, by Schubert and by Joseph Lanner.

One of the most common *style hongrois* fiddle techniques is pizzicato; an instance of this was already seen in example 9d, from the Haydn Trio's "Gipsy" finale. The Hungarian poet and military officer Joseph Gvadányi (1725–1801), for example, remarked upon both the string plucking and the rich ornamentation of the Gypsies' style,[2] and the tradition was probably a very old one even then. Indeed, it could well predate the Gypsies' entry onto the Hungarian musical scene. Julius Kaldy pointed out that the traditional Hungarian lute was played pizzicato (as opposed to, perhaps, strumming) and cited the presence of the fiddle at this early stage of Hungarian musical development.[3] (The key point here is not which instrument was played in a plucked style, but that such a technique was an important part of Hungarian instrumental practice.) As a matter of fact, Kaldy also stated that by the sixteenth century the Gypsies were already playing the fiddle with a bow; this implies that some time before it had been done otherwise, although it is hard to imagine plucking as a primary method of playing a fiddlelike instrument.

The excerpt in example 19, taken from Liszt's eighth Hungarian Rhapsody, illustrates another characteristic and much-noted aspect of Gypsy playing. This music had tremendous rhythmic flexibility; the maintenance of group ensemble without a restrictive beat or a time-beating conductor (both of which were studiously avoided) was both marvelous and inexplicable to all who witnessed it. One of the most breathless passages from Liszt's book describes this phenomenon thus:

Example 18. Rude, violinistic "double stops."

18a. Schubert, Piano Sonata in D Major, D. 850, I, mm. 48–52.

18b. Lanner, *Ungarischer Nationaltanz,* op. 168, mm. 49–52.

Example 19. Liszt, *Hungarian Rhapsody* no. 8, m. 40.

The habit of ornamentation . . . elevates the first violin to the position of principal personage in the orchestra. . . . It is the first violin who decides the degree of movement; and, as soon as he has embarked on any special feature, the orchestra waits in silence for the emotion to subside. The extent of his expression depends entirely upon the inspiration of the moment; which also decides the precise form to be given to the cloud of notes. These roll forth in example after example, remindful of the entangled tendrils, the tear drops from which in autumn are as the notes of melody falling one by one.

The orchestra is so electrified by the fire, or, it may be, the melancholy of its chief, that, when the latter has come to the end of his explorations—when, having allowed himself sufficiently long to float in air, he gives the sign of being about to fall, they never fail to share his emotion. When, therefore, the moment arrives for receiving him into their arms they do not allow him to reach the earth, but sustain him, aid him to rebound.[4]

The left-hand chord at the end of this excerpt shows just this usage: the stylized "orchestra" is clearly intended to catch the soloist at the end of his "improvisation" without the slightest feeling of metric constraint or insecurity. This is, of course, easiest to simulate with one pianist; ensemble *style hongrois* pieces generally do not try for this effect because the magical Gypsy ensemble would too likely be found to be lacking in players inexperienced with the idiom.

Even more than the ensemble aspect, Liszt obviously takes great joy in describing the Gypsies' ornamentation itself. Elsewhere, he says:

> It was the Bohemian virtuosi who festooned Bohemian melody with their florid ornaments seeming to throw upon each, as it were, the prism of a rainbow or the scintillation of a multi-colored sash.[5]

Further,

> This flowery ornamentation disports itself as promiscuously as if it were a flight of butterflies; sometimes lively and joyous, rapid and rebounding like a dancer who rhythmically outlines a melody while seeming scarcely to touch the ground; yet sometimes slow and monotonous as if depressed. The bunches of notes fall in abundance as if running over the brim of a horn of plenty. At each organ-point they are like myriads of sparkling atoms, as if an odorous rain had converted itself into a vaporous drapery by which we had become enveloped; or like the snowy foam of a wave which rises like an amorous water-nymph.[6]

And again,

> The masters of Bohemian art, eminently inspired, will not submit to any laws of reflection or restraint;

proceeding spontaneously and until now inseparably from improvisation. They give free course to every caprice and turn of fancy; gallop across country whilst indulging in endless transformations of the same material; or they saunter along a meandering path, giving to zig-zags an unexpected movement and allowing the imagination freely to suggest the many forms of embellishment known collectively as arabesque.[7]

And yet again,

> In the next place the true Bohemian master never accepts a song or dance motive except either as the text of his discourse, or as the epigraph of a poem. This idea is one of which he never loses sight and upon which he is prepared to expatiate simply without end. The master most to be admired is he who enriches his theme with such a profusion of traits (appoggiaturas, tremolos, scales, arpeggios and diatonic or chromatic passages) that under this luxuriant embroidery the primitive thought appears no more prominently than the fabric of his garment appears upon his sleeve, peeping through the lacework which artistically hides it by its closeness of design.
>
> But, like the fabric, the melody dare not disappear; for it is the stuff or material which sustains the form.[8]

These loving descriptions of the ornamentation highlight what may be the most remarked-upon aspect of Hungarian-Gypsy music making, that also cited by Gvadányi. The virtuosity of *friss* playing notwithstanding, Gypsy ornamentation is most closely associated with slow music. In the slow instrumental style, called *hallgató* (as described in chapter 1), the role of ornamentation is one of expression more than display, and the *nóta* songs that traditionally formed the basis of *hallgató* improvisations are entirely divorced from textual meaning and rhythm. As Sárosi describes,

> On their instruments they can perform a *hallgató* melody—which normally has a text—much more

loosely, like an instrumental fantasy, and working *against* the dictates of the text; with runs, touching, languid pauses, and sustained or snapped off notes, they virtually pull the original structure apart.[9] [my emphasis]

He points out that the original character of the songs is lost in such performances, and that the rubato-style performances of the Gypsies have so shaped audience taste that any other approach sounds out of place. Indeed, a more faithful, non-*hallgató* rendition of the song would be contrary to the essential character of the style. Compare Liszt's comments on this phenomenon:

When these melodies are merely sung, they are in the state of being deprived of their variegated plumage, as well as of the thousand facets presented by a profuse ornamentation.[10]

But it is here that the musician's contribution comes into play in "creating" this rubato style. The motivation of Gypsy *style hongrois* performances is and always was commercial: the musicians play whatever the customer wants to pay for. In the Gypsy performance tradition, the soloist looks into a customer's soul, (supposedly) perceives and understands his personal sorrows and concerns, and expresses them on his instrument. When the Gypsy "plays" the customer's deepest feelings, the customer then feels as if he or she has an integral part in the composition.

Example 8, given in chapter 3, gives one of the clearest early examples of stylized *hallgató* writing: a Haydn quartet adagio that features slow-moving chords under a shower of free ornamentation from the first violin (the theme being maintained in the second violin). But *hallgató* writing was not the exclusive province of the fiddle; middle-range woodwinds also had a long tradition of this kind of expression. Example

20, the middle section of the second movement from Brahms's Clarinet Quintet op. 115, gives a clarinet's-eye-view of this style: bursts of notes, turning figures, and runs accompanied by crying string figures. The woodwind soloist in the *style hongrois* is subsidiary to the fiddler, but nonetheless important and present in many evocations of Gypsy playing. This excerpt, and the remarks quoted in chapter 4 about the Gypsies' excellence in wind music, point up its importance for them. It may well be the result of a Gypsy tradition older than that of the fiddle.

Example 20. Brahms, Clarinet Quintet, op. 115, II, middle section.

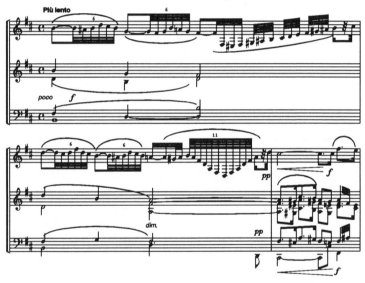

In the *style hongrois*, a solo clarinet or oboe is a reminiscence of the *tárogató*, a shrill, shawmlike instrument that dates back to the Hungarian independence movement of the late seventeenth century, although there is no record of a role for it in the early Gypsy bands. There is also a more clarinetlike instrument called the *Schunda tárogató*, invented in 1896 as more or less a Romantic evocation of the earlier instrument.[11] Seemingly, the woodwind sound and the instrument's role are more important than the actual instrument, as the *Schunda tárogató* achieved no lasting place in this style, while in general the clarinet maintained its position of prominence. The Brahms passage in example 20 is one example of this; another is given in example 21, from the second movement of the Schubert "Great" C Major Symphony (D. 944), where an oboe soloist provides a shrill, exotic melody of clearly Hungarian character (this will be even clearer when we survey the characteristic rhythms of the *style hongrois*).

Example 21. Schubert, "Great" Symphony in C Major, D. 944, II, mm. 160–66.

The situation of the bagpipe is similar to that of the *tárogató*. Bagpipes were favored by Gypsy musicians in the era before the Gypsy bands, either played solo or perhaps accompanying a fiddle, but the instrument never became a necessary part of the larger Gypsy ensemble. Bagpipe playing has now all but died out in its original Hungarian context, but certain characteristics of the bagpipers' style live on: melodies within the range of an octave, for example, and drone fifths. In the *style hongrois*, these low fifths remained; in the Gypsy bands they would have been played by a double bass rather than a bagpipe, but the sound remained. Liszt provides a description of this characteristic:

> Among the Gipsies of Moldowallachia the spiritual and stimulating principle of the Hungarian Gipsy melody is held in check by the continuous use of the pedal-bass. Moreover, this organ-point effect is invariably limited to the tonic; which holds the harmony in such a condition of servitude that it is, as it were, painfully attached to the soil.[12]

We already saw one example of prominently placed drone fifths in the Mozart string quartet finale in example 11 (chapter 3), and example 22 gives two Schubertian instances: bagpipelike parallel fifths from the String Quintet in C Major (D. 956) and static drone fifths from the *Divertissement à l'Hongroise* (D. 818). (Note that in 22a, the example from the quintet, the ensemble catches and cradles the unison line with an effect very like that of example 19.)

One instrument the Hungarian-Gypsy bands did not share with musicians further west was the cimbalom. This malleted string instrument is of Hungarian derivation and is central to Gypsy bands as both soloist and accompanist. Initially it had no sustaining pedal, and although it acquired one by the middle-to-late nineteenth century, this pedal was still a rela-

Example 22. Drone fifths.

22a. Schubert, String Quintet in C Major, D. 956, trio from III.

22b. Schubert, *Divertissement à l'Hongroise,* D. 818, I, mm. 70–71 (reduction).

tively crude device. Cimbalom evocations on the piano involve frequent use of the sustaining pedal, and even occasional blending of harmony. Liszt offers a colorful, romantic picture of the cimbalom's multifaceted role:

> The *zymbala* supplies the rhythm, indicates the acceleration or slackening of time, and also the degree of movement. He manipulates with singular agility and as if it were a sleight-of-hand performance the little wooden hammers with which he travels over the strings, and which in this primitive piano perform the duty we assign to ivory keys.
>
> The *zymbala* shares with the first violin the right to develop certain passages and to prolong certain variations indefinitely according to the good pleasure of the moment. He is necessarily one of those who conduct the musical poem; having either created it at leisure, or being about to improvise it at the moment; and he imposes upon others the duty of surrounding him, sustaining him, even guessing him in order to sing the same funereal hymn or give himself up to the same mad freak of joy.[13]

Liszt's piano music provides the best examples of stylized cimbaloms: example 23 shows three different personalities of the instrument—harmonic (23a), declamatory (23b), and vir-

Example 23. Cimbalom evocations by Liszt.

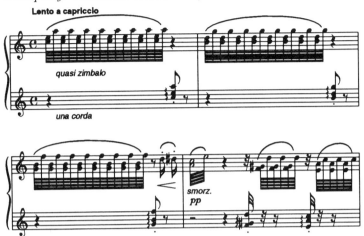

23a. *Hungarian Rhapsody* no. 11, opening.

23b. *Hungarian Rhapsody* no. 12, opening.

23c. Hungarian Fantasia, vivace section.

tuosic (23c). Other composers, such as Schubert, frequently used tremolo effects in *style hongrois* pieces, and these seem to be evocations of the softly thrumming cimbalom as well.

The human voice is evoked by two separate *style hongrois* gestures. This is a unique situation because vocal music per se has never been important in the Hungarian-Gypsy performances, and what these gestures represent is stylized imitations of the Gypsies' *instrumental* imitations of the voice. That is, these two aspects of the *style hongrois* copy gestures that were imitations to begin with. Clearly, both were native to particular districts in eastern Europe, where the Gypsies would have encountered them. The first of these, grace notes of more than a fifth above the principal note, are recognizable by American audiences from recent performances and recordings by the Bulgarian State Radio and Television Female Vocal Choir. Often, but not always, this figure functions as a struck suspension of the previous note when the melody suddenly drops. One example of this was shown in example 16a, in m. 14 of Hummel's first *Ballo Ongaro;* another, shown in example 24, is from Schubert's *Divertissement à l'Hongroise.*

Example 24. Schubert, *Divertissement à l'Hongroise*, III, mm. 113–20 (reduction).

The second originally vocal characteristic is the crying, heavily doubled parallel thirds and sixths. This is descended from parallel-interval folk-music styles in central and eastern Europe and differs in balance from traditional western harmonic thirds and sixths. Neither pitch is "the melody"; they are equal, and the result is a rough, keening quality (imitating the folk practice), far more appropriate to this context than is sweetness and subtle voicing. (This, too, is a facet of performances by the Bulgarian Female Choir, but they also sing in parallel seconds, sevenths, and ninths.) One example of this was already seen in the string accompaniment to the clarinet solo in Brahms's Clarinet Quintet (see example 20); another is seen in example 25, from Brahms's Hungarian Dance no. 5.

Example 25. Brahms, *Hungarian Dance* no. 5, mm. 41–44 (reduction).

Rhythms. Another large group of gestures associated with the *style hongrois* is rhythmic. Some of these are derived from the Hungarian language, the original text of the *nóta* songs, and they lend a strange and angular feel to instrumental music, particularly when they are coupled with uneven phrasing. Others are traditional ornamental rhythms, valued by Gypsy instrumentalists for their liveliness and effect. Many are peculiar to the *style hongrois;* a few are not, but are recurrent parts of the language. In general, the metaphor of a specific musical dialect seems clearest when discussing rhythmic gestures, because these are the gestures that most clearly stand out in relief from a busy texture or thick instrumentation.

The spondee, a metric foot consisting of two longs, is a common Hungarian reference. One example was shown in example 21, from the Schubert "Great," and another is seen in example 26, the closing theme to the first movement of Schubert's C major string quintet. This rhythm can either begin a phrase or end one, but its sudden, accented suspension of quicker motion has an unmistakable punctuating effect. Another metrical foot used in the *style hongrois* and avoided elsewhere is the choriambus, long-short-short-long. Two examples are shown in example 27, from Liszt's *Hungar-*

ian Fantasia and from Joseph Joachim's Hungarian Violin Concerto. The rhythmic notation differs slightly between the two examples; Joachim's, in which the first short is longer than the second, is perhaps closer to the original inflection. Indeed, in a recent recording of the *Fantasia* by Jorge Bolet it is this second realization that is played in the orchestra, despite Liszt's rhythmically more straitened notation. We in the twentieth century commonly see this rhythm in the works of Bartók, particularly in the folksong settings, which underscores its connection with the Hungarian language.

Example 26. Schubert, String Quintet in C Major, D. 956, I, mm. 138–46.

Example 27. The choriambus.

27a. Liszt, *Hungarian Fantasia,* principal theme.

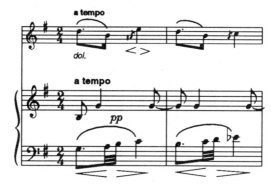

27b. Joachim, Hungarian Violin Concerto in D Minor, op. 11, II, mm. 11–12.

The accented short-long is another characteristic figure, one which is essentially the same as the medieval "Lombard" rhythm. Examples of this abound; two are shown in example 28. One of the clearest examples of an angular rhythm turned graceful is seen in the Brahms passage, while the Lanner gives a different view of the possibilities. Another angular feature is the Hungarian anapest, accented short-short-long, which also occurs with frequency. Example 29 gives two examples, one from Hummel and another from Weber.

The *alla zoppa* (Italian, "limping") rhythm is one of the most common in the *style hongrois*. It consists of a quarter

Example 28. The Lombard rhythm.

28a. Brahms, *Hungarian Dance* no. 17, mm. 61–64 (reduction).

28b. Lanner, *Ungarischer Nationaltanz,* op. 168, mm. 91–92.

note between two eighth notes, or a half note flanked by quarters. In melodic uses, the syncopation marks itself for attention by virtue of the sudden stop, and in faster music, it produces a highly infectious and kinetic dance rhythm. One example of the melodic *alla zoppa* appeared in example 26, and a famous example of dancing-song *alla zoppa* use appears in example 30.

Example 29. The Hungarian anapest.

29a. Hummel, *Ballo Ongaro* no. 7, mm. 9–12.

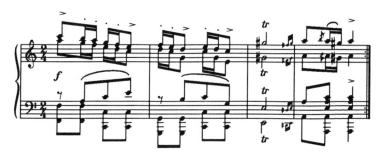

29b. Weber, *Alla Zingara* piano duet movement from op. 60, mm. 27–30 (reduction).

A very common ornamental rhythm in the *style hongrois* was the dotted rhythm, most often dotted eighth-sixteenth. This was all but universal in *verbunkos* and was a staple of Gypsy fiddlers as it provided an insinuating, attractive swing to melodies.[14] We have already seen this characteristic in examples 17, 21, and 26. Another rhythm by no means unique to the *style hongrois* but ubiquitous within it is the simple decorative triplet. For this I have no particular explanation except to say that Gypsy fiddlers must have used it constantly, to judge by its use in Hungarian-influenced pieces. Passages shown in example 31, taken from among many, are by Schumann and Schubert.

Characteristics such as the triplet and dotted rhythm pose a special problem because they are ubiquitous in works

Example 30. Schubert, String Quintet in C Major, D. 956, IV, opening.

designated as *hongrois* or *zingarese* but are also plentiful in other styles. They therefore cannot in and of themselves be understood as certain indications of the style's presence. In cases where there is no explicit titular or characteristic designation, it is safe to expect at least three different gestures from the style; one of these ornamental figures in conjunction with, say, an obvious drone fifth and *alla zoppa* syncopations is unquestionably a characteristic of the *style hongrois*, whereas simple triplets or dotted rhythms in the minor mode might as easily represent ornamentation in the Italian virtuoso violin style. Obviously, some aspects of the *style hongrois* stand out in greater relief than others, so while spondees or cimbalom

Example 31. Ornamental triplets.

31a. Schumann, *Sonata for the Young*, op. 117/3, III: *Zigeunertanz*, opening.

31b. Schubert, *Divertissement à l'Hongroise*, III, 241–45.

imitations might singlehandedly evoke the Hungarian Gypsies, with other gestures the immediate musical environment
takes on greater importance.

The *bókazó* rhythm is one of the clearest indications of the
style hongrois, and is often called the *bókazó* cadence because
of its frequent appearance at the end of phrases. So common

is it in this style that Liszt referred to it simply as the "Magyar cadence." Its origins are well known: meaning "capering," the *bókazó* rhythm comes from a traditional heel- and spur-clicking figure common to Hungarian dance. We saw one example of this rhythm in the accompaniment in example 21; example 32 gives two more versions of it, one each from Schubert and Liszt. The gravity of traditional Hungarian dance, the explicit importance (discussed in chapter 1) given to the spur-clicking step, and the Hungarians' history as an equestrian people help to explain the significance of this figure and its role in the *style hongrois*.

Melodic gestures. The *bókazó* figure is a special case in that usually it is not only a rhythm but also a specific melodic

Example 32. The *bókazó* rhythm.

32a. Schubert, *Divertissement à l'Hongroise,* I, m. 21.

32b. Liszt, *Hungarian Rhapsody* no. 3, mm. 13–14.

contour associated with it: a turn beginning with the upper neighbor. Example 21, where the rhythm serves as background to the return of the main theme in the second movement of the Schubert "Great," is something of an exception in this regard. However, this figure is only one of a family of melodic *style hongrois* gestures, gestures that are either specific melodic figures or simply idiosyncratic modal sequences of intervals.

The most obvious is the interval of the augmented second. This is probably the only musical charactericstic to have survived from the period before the Gypsies came even as far west as Hungary. It is not known in originally Hungarian music, and seems to come from Turkey and lands east, where it is a common melodic interval. The Gypsies happily insert it anywhere possible, whether it was part of the original melody or not, because their audiences love the highly colored, exotic effect. Further, there is at least the theoretical existence of the "Gypsy Scale," which is based on the augmented second as an expressive device.

The music the Gypsies performed was widely assumed to conform to this peculiar scale, although it is clear that in reality there was no such restriction and that major and minor scales were also common. Indeed, there is some disagreement as to what the scale (or mode) actually was. James Huneker, one of Liszt's early biographers, describes it as a harmonic minor scale with a raised fourth degree (see example 33), but he says that others read the same pitch sequence differently by starting on the dominant, which results in a major scale with a flatted second and sixth.[15] The noteworthy aspect of this interval sequence is, obviously, the fact that it has two augmented seconds in it, and as Sárosi has pointed out the augmented second is a virtual requirement of any Gypsy performance, regardless of whether the original melody uses it or not.[16] It is really an inflection, an aspect of the Gypsy performance "accent," rather than a sign of some kind of a Rom-specific scale, and is thus analagous to the interpolation of "blue notes" in twentieth-century blues interpretations of popular songs. To the popular mind the augmented second represents the essence of Gypsy melody, so although the scale was really a latter-day theoretical construct, it remains associated with the idea of Gypsy performances. It is certainly likely that, even though there was no formalized scale from the Gypsies' point of view, the end result of many Gypsy performances probably corresponded to that sequence of intervals. Moreover, an exponent of the *style hongrois* such as Liszt took its existence for granted and discussed it in his book. The "Gypsy Scale," then, finally must be understood to have some kind of real existence, even if it did not derive from the earliest disseminators of Hungarian-Gypsy music.

Example 33. The "Gypsy Scale," showing its identically configured fourths.

Another melodic feature of the *style hongrois* is the raised fourth degree in major mode. I hesitate to call it a Lydian fourth for two reasons: the perfect fourth is also frequently present in the same context, which it cannot be in the traditional Lydian mode,[17] and it might simply be the remains of the Gypsy scale once the mode has switched from minor to major. In any case, the raised fourth tends to lend importance to the fifth degree by acting as a kind of secondary leading tone, and to give melodies a glistening, transparent sound. Two instances of this were already seen in examples 10c and 22b; example 34 gives a sample by Liszt.

One melodic figure is, even in the absence of any other

Example 34. Liszt, *Hungarian Rhapsody* no. 9, mm. 20–21.

characteristics of the *style hongrois,* an unmistakable indication of Hungarian subject matter: the so-called *Kuruc*-fourth, a rebounding figure that alternates between the fifth scale degree and upper prime. This figure, the opening gesture of the famous *Rákóczi Song* (ancestor of the more famous *Rákóczi March*),[18] dates back to the *Kuruc* period of the late seventeenth century; when it is sounded it evokes great feelings of Hungarian national pride. A clear explanation of its significance appears in a letter of 1881 from Alexander Borodin to Cesar Cui, in which Borodin describes sitting with Liszt at a rehearsal of Liszt's *Coronation Mass.* Liszt leaned over to Borodin in the course of the rehearsal and explained "that the use of [melodic] fourths constitutes a characteristic feature of Hungarian music."[19] We have already seen a Mozartean deployment of this important figure in m. 137 of example 12a and a small Haydnesque use in m. 10 of example 8. Example 35 gives three more instances: first, a Liszt passage in which it appears close to its original form, in a quotation of *Rákóczi Song;* second, an excerpt from Liszt's setting of Nicholas Lenau's poem *Drei Zigeuner* on the line "and his cimbalom hung on a tree"; and third, an example from Schubert.

Harmony. Some of the most striking effects in the entire *style hongrois* are caused by a nonfunctional deployment of harmony, one that features sudden chordal shifts and juxtapositions of distant chords. Here is a description from Liszt's book:[20]

Example 35. The *Kuruc*-fourth.

35a. Liszt, *Hungarian Fantasia, hallgató* section.

35b. Liszt, *Drei Zigeuner,* mm. 68–70.

35c. Schubert, *Fantasie* in F Minor for piano four-hands, D. 940, mm. 1–4 (reduction).

> In his music [the Gypsy] revealed that golden ray of interior light proper to himself, which otherwise the world would never have known or suspected. He made it dance and glitter in the fascination of a wild harmony, fantastic and full of discords; and thus, by a mixture of unexpected outline, glaring colour, sudden change and quick transformation, endowed it with its many seductive features.[21]

It may be that such harmonic effects were a natural outgrowth of a folklike repertoire that was primarily modal; after all, where melodies are not strongly functional, there is no reason for the accompaniment to be. Another plausible explanation is ignorance; Sárosi has suggested that harmonic audacities in, for example, Liszt's Hungarian Rhapsodies "idealize rather than imitate the one-time clumsiness of Gypsy harmonization."[22] Regardless of their origin, such effects, with their elements of surprise and their vivid coloring, have long been associated with Gypsy performances. Liszt's book stresses the Gypsies' "habit of passing suddenly to a remote key," and that their "system of modulation seems to be based on a total negation of all predetermined plan for the purpose in question."[23] Clearly, Hungarian-Gypsy harmonic practice depended on motivations other than "functionality."

In Liszt's view, the Gypsies' harmonic practices are directly related to the peculiarities of the Gypsy scale, and his explanation for this gleefully overstates the response of schooled musicians to these musical characteristics. Here are two separate passages:

> The civilised musician is at first so astounded by the strangeness of the intervals employed in Bohemian music that he can find no other way of settling the matter in his own mind than that of concluding the dissonances to be accidental; that they are mere inexactitudes; or, to be quite frank, faults of execution. He is equally put out

by the modulations; which are habitually so abrupt as to defy his most treasured scientific musical tenets. If he could make up his mind to take them seriously at all they would horrify and scandalise him; and he would probably consider their position in musical art as about equivalent to rape, strangulation or parricide.[24]

> Bohemian music with few exceptions adopts, for its minor scale, the augmented fourth, diminished sixth and augmented seventh. By the augmentation of the fourth, especially, the harmony acquires a strangely dazzling character—a brilliancy resulting only in obscurity. Every musician recognises at once how decidedly and to what an extent this practically constant triple modification of the intervals caused the harmony of Gipsy music to differ from that in use by us.[25]

It is, of course, amusing to see trained musicians scorned in one passage and then deferentially cited in the second. However, making allowances for terminology—he can only mean minor sixth and major seventh—Liszt does identify something important. When a melody's prevailing intervallic structure highlights scale degrees different from those stressed in more familiar music, idiosyncratic modulations are less surprising. Note, for example, the emphasis on the fifth scale degree in the Gypsy Scale. It has half-steps resolving to it from both above and below (a privilege not accorded even to the tonic), and the peculiar intervallic series below it (semitone-augmented second-semitone) is the same as that below the tonic. In cases where the *Kuruc*-fourth is used, that figure rebounds between the fifth and prime scale degrees in such a way as to tonicize either; indeed, the usual rhythm (dotted, long note on the fifth degree) seems to make the fifth sound more reposeful. Certainly, this does not account for many other striking harmonic effects in the *style hongrois,* many of which are based on thirds or more distant intervals, rather than on fourths and fifths. It does illustrate, though, the relationship between melodic and harmonic configurations, and how a peculiar intervallic arrangement can lend itself to atypical harmonic practices when trained musicians are using it in a "semifunctional" manner to evoke an untrained, nonfunctional, "vernacular" style.

One example of the wildest kind of brusque harmonic practice appears in example 22a, the trio from the third movement of a Schubert string quintet. The previous section, an unbridled, drone-filled scherzo, has just ended with a firm C major cadence. In a sudden switch to profound pathos, the trio begins in the parallel minor and in six bars has travelled to D-flat major, through a reference to the subdominant of G-flat major. As if this were not distant enough, there is an immediate reference to G-flat *minor* following. A more prosaic example is found in Lanner's *Ungarischer Nationaltanz,* which simply juxtaposes chords a third from each other in a jarring way (as shown in example 36). But the passage that is undoubtedly the tour-de-force evocation of Gypsy harmonic use is shown in example 37. This lengthy excerpt from the third movement of Schubert's *Divertissement à l'Hongroise* begins in a soft and somewhat threatening F-sharp minor (with strumming cimbaloms in the background), has a sudden and eye-wateringly angelic passage in the parallel major (mm. 296–303), and then suddenly cadences in C-sharp minor. After the double bar, sudden slamming G major chords lead to C major, followed by A chords leading to D major, and B minor chords leading to E minor; only then does the section finally subside back to F-sharp minor and the same threatening cimbalom tremolo from the opening.

What makes this passage so masterful is its suggestion of furious, mercurial mood shifts, one after the other. From the smouldering F-sharp minor cimbaloms, through the almost unbearably poignant F-sharp major passage, to the unbridled, almost furious rejoicing of the following chord changes, each new harmony suggests a new emotional state.

Example 36. Lanner, *Ungarischer Nationaltanz,* op. 168, mm. 79–83.

Perhaps it is here that much of the power of the Hungarian-Gypsy idiom really comes into focus. The allure was not merely the titillation of shocking harmonic changes, or that the dance rhythms were a veritable command to get up and move. Those attractive aspects were certainly there and were no doubt sufficient for many listeners. But on a deeper level, one could look at societal outcasts performing this music and hear an almost too-desperate celebration, a bottomless grief, and a wild, kaleidoscopic shifting between moods with no attempt at (or desire for) transition between them. This music came to suggest the condition of those who played it and thus was a constant reminder of society's mixed feelings about the Gypsies, of the fear and revulsion, envy and attraction.

When the *style hongrois* is discussed by Hungarian musicologists (Sárosi and Szabolcsi, for example), it seems to be taken for granted that the reader has a good idea of what is being discussed and that there would be no benefit to setting out each convention. Part of the reason for this is that in most cases a Hungarian and perhaps German readership is intended

Example 37. Schubert, *Divertissement à l'Hongroise,* mm. 288–325.

(such later translations as appear being largely serendipitous), so that some native familiarity with the gestures of the dialect is assumed. The fact is, the *style hongrois* now has much less immediacy than it did when people heard Gypsy performers much more often, when they lived near Gypsies and saw their circumstances, and when the stereotypes were an active part of the popular culture. Once we establish our lexicon, we have taken a first step; we can now establish when the dialect is being spoken and can proceed to considerations of how, why, and with what intent it is being used.

The *style hongrois* in the nineteenth century, however, had more complex resonances than those explainable by a knowledge of the Gypsies and their musical gestures and idiosyncratic performance style. They and their music could be used by different composers to represent different extramusical ideas. It would be a gross misrepresentation to suggest that when Schubert or Liszt, to choose two examples, wrote in the *style hongrois,* they were merely availing themselves of an increasingly popular vernacular music disseminated by exotic musicians of foreign extraction. Each of the composers who used this dialect with the greatest command, freedom, and conviction made it an individual, personal language, suitable to his own purposes. This is not surprising; we would not expect major compositional figures to make the choice of musical language for a piece, movement, or passage capriciously. But proceeding from the (in my opinion, valid) assumption that the decision to use the *style hongrois* would not have been based on a mere whim, our task now is to examine the intent behind its best uses. In other words, we have some idea of the sound of this vernacular, and of its compound gestures; we must now strive to understand its deeper meanings.

PART TWO

Introduction to Part Two

THERE WERE four composers who used the *style hongrois* with unique command and eloquence: Carl Maria von Weber, Franz Schubert, Franz Liszt, and Johannes Brahms. In the lifetimes of Weber and Schubert it was an emerging popular style, Liszt saw it flower into maturity, and by Brahms's time it was both ubiquitous and traditional, rather (one suspects) like the hyper-Romantic musical language of Hollywood film is today. The popularity of the works of two of these figures, Liszt and Brahms, is almost solely responsible for the fact that we remember the *style hongrois* at all.

For three of these cases the dialect eventually took on associations far beyond those of simple "characteristic" music. These deeper meanings can best be understood by examining the context in which the style was used, the composers' own lives and how these works related to them, and by remembering what we have already seen about the Gypsy stereotypes and position in society. No music is heard in a cultural vacuum; a musical language with vivid and compelling extramusical associations cannot be completely understood in purely musical terms.

In contrast, the legions of minor masters using the *style hongrois* were more likely simply to be exploiting a musical fad, which beyond a doubt it was fast becoming. To choose two examples from among many, Ferdinand Ries's *Variations on a Hungarian Theme* (op. 15, 1819) and Lanner's *Ungarische Nationaltanz* (op. 168, 183–?), do not seem to be heartfelt statements in a specifically chosen musical language but instead somewhat superficial uses of an increasingly popular music. As we saw earlier, such music had enjoyed commercial popularity since the 1780s.

I do not mean to imply that major figures automatically used the *style hongrois* in a profound way, as distinguished from *Kleinmeister,* who were equally automatically grinding out drivel. Robert Schumann, for example, included a *Zigeunertanz* movement (which we encountered briefly in chapter 5) in one of his sonatas for the young; it is entirely undistinguished and forgettable, despite coming from the pen of one of the most imaginative tone poets of the nineteenth century. On the other hand, the *Hausmusik* could achieve a very high quality. We already saw the cleverness of Hummel's *Balli Ongaresi,* and the much later suite *Tziganyi* by Stephen Heller (op. 138, nos. 16–20) expertly captures the Hungarian-Gypsy ambience, with the intermediate pianist, not the virtuoso, in mind.

Nonetheless, these four major figures attain a unique kind of expression using this dialect. For three of them, the impetus to use this vernacular was not that it enabled them to cash in on something commercially viable, but that it gave them access to a kind of expression unavailable in the prevailing musical language. In the case of Brahms, through sheer mastery of the style he was able to elevate it out of the *Hausmusik* realm entirely, even while writing for precisely that market. Taken as a group, the four stand far above the majority using this vernacular tongue. An examination of their works, therefore, will result in a better understanding of the role of the *style hongrois* in its greater nineteenth-century context.

CHAPTER 6

Weber

CARL MARIA VON WEBER (1786–1826), in addition to being one of the founding fathers of Romantic music, was a composer thoroughly familiar with the musical language and conventions of the eighteenth century. He acquired his knowledge of earlier music young, as it was essentially the family business. His parents had been musicians and theater performers, Mozart's wife, Constanze *(née* Weber), and her sister Aloysia, an opera singer, were his second cousins, and he even had a period of study, at age ten, with the sixty-year-old Michael Haydn, who (although somewhat in eclipse now) was a major figure to his Classical contemporaries. One of the clearest examples of an eighteenth-century approach in Weber's music is the Turkish opera *Abu Hassan* (1810–11): this work dates from well after the "Turkish" craze, but is nonetheless firmly within its genre in terms of satiric character types and musical idiom.

Yet, his theatrical instincts were too sure to limit him to the conventions of a musical language that had essentially ceased to develop. Throughout Weber's work there is a folklike, vernacular sensibility foreign to the mature Classicists; an almost naïve frankness was replacing wit, and this put his music into a different aesthetic realm altogether. Some of this approach could have stemmed from the Abbé Vogler, with whom Weber studied in 1803 and 1804; Vogler had exposed him to the world of folksongs and folk poetry and to the idea that these represented a kind of unspoiled People's Art.[1] Weber was receptive to this message; moreover, his connections with the folk tradition and its source material went beyond the purely musical. In 1813 he formed friendships with Ludwig Achim von Arnim and Clemens Brentano, the brothers-in-law who assembled and published the folktale collection *Des Knaben Wunderhorn* (1805) and whose Gypsy tales we touched on in chapter 4. The use of a folk-based musical language may also have had practical advantages: given Weber's lack of long-term financial security, it was advisable to keep well in touch with popular taste and with those styles and ideas that would produce a favorable public response.

As might be expected of a composer attuned to musical vernaculars, he composed several instrumental works in the *style hongrois*. The earliest of these is the *Andante und Rondo ungarese* for viola and orchestra, composed for Fritz, his brother, in 1809; he later arranged the solo part for bassoon. This is a charming and effective work, in which a C minor *Andante*, displaying both moodiness and an obvious joy in the display of florid *passagio*, is answered by an *Allegretto ungarese* replete with characteristic rhythms and a large measure of dash and virtuosity. The year 1816 saw the *Sieben Variationen über ein Zigeunerlied*, a commissioned work lacking, unfortunately, both an interesting theme and any demonstrable commitment on the part of the composer. In 1819 Weber completed the *Huit pièces* for piano duet, the fourth of which was entitled *Alla Zingara* (an excerpt appeared in chapter 5). Here again is a delightful Hungarian-Gypsy essay, decidedly of the *Hausmusik* variety but no less a success on that account. Hungarian rhythms, frequent and prominent thirds and sixths, and bursts of runs in sixteenth notes make this an attractive romp, although after the first page the secondo part is largely relegated to an accompanying role.

Were his output in the *style hongrois* limited to these few works, little would be proven other than his awareness of the style and that his facility for musical vernaculars such as the Turkish Style and German *Singverein* idiom carried over to this one as well. But Weber composed for the theater perhaps more naturally than for any other circumstance, and it is in the theatrical music that his expression can seem least fettered. One of his dramatic works is based on a story involving Gypsies, and another contains subtle references to their musical language. It is in these works that, I believe, the *style hongrois* began to acquire meanings past the obvious and superficial. For the explicitly Gypsy story, we must return to Cervantes' *La Gitanilla*.

As mentioned in chapter 4, among all the imputed Gypsy vices this tale dwells only upon theft; so while not being overly complimentary it is not as malicious as many other sources. Cervantes' Gypsies are loyal to one another, clever, and adroit. If the work can be taken to represent any kind of popular image, then in Spain the essence of the Gypsy stereotype was something between nuisance and tolerated outsider, but nothing like what it would become—clear menace, present danger—in eighteenth-century Germany. Many more negative stereotypes would surface in the story when Cervantes' work was rendered into German by Pius Alexander Wolff.

Wolff (1782–1828), a student of Goethe, was a successful

actor and sometime dramatist Weber had first known and admired in Berlin. He had written a prose play based on Cervantes' story, retitled *Preciosa,* that had enjoyed some success when produced in Leipzig in 1811 with music by Traugott Eberwein. Although the play had also been set by two other composers, Wolff still saw fit to rework it and after finishing a version in verse approached Weber to provide the music.[2]

The story, as we saw in chapter 4, is uncomplicated and makes for an ideal dramatic vehicle. As a starting point, Gypsies in Spain provide a colorful backdrop of strangers in an already exotic setting. The virtuous, clever Preciosa would charm even the hardest heart and her suitor, Andrés, could move mountains with his fidelity and sacrifice for his beloved. In Wolff's adaptation of the work for German audiences, though, the character of the Gypsies is thoroughly trans-formed.

Initially, the Gypsies seem benign, and Wolff presents them not merely as travellers but as nature worshippers. This gives Weber the opportunity to provide music of a typical "out-door" type, full of fanfare figures and horn fifths. Here are two verses from the Gypsy chorus that opens Act II, trans-lated literally:

> In the wood, the wood,
> In the fresh, green wood,
> Where an echo sounds,
> Here song sounds and horns ring,
> So merrily though the silent forest
> Tra-ra, Tra-ra [etc.]
>
> . . . .
>
> The world, the world,
> The great, wide world is our tent.
> The winds resound and, singing,
> We wander the woods, valleys, and rocky cliffs.
> Halloh! Halloh![3]

Another bow to German dramatic convention is the exaggeration of the love interest. The attraction to Preciosa felt by a young knight, here called Don Alonzo rather than Andrès, and her reciprocal feelings (which were only hinted at by Cervantes), become in Wolff's hands an excuse for tedious dramatic filler. The other Gypsies leave them alone, giving him the opportunity to pledge his love in a stock romance scene. She cannot believe her ears but responds, openly calling him her friend, and so forth. When Alonzo goes before the Gypsy chieftain to pledge his commitment to her and to follow the Gypsy tribe, the chieftain says, by way of welcome, explanation, and introduction:

> We're a friendly people
> We wander the world without worry;
> What we need, we have,
> Because we are satisfied with very little.
>
> .   .   .   .
>
> Good, true mother earth,
> Our cradle, our grave![4]

The emphasis to this point is on happy, nature-loving wanderers, not on robbing or misdeeds. Beginning with the third act, however, Wolff departs radically from Cervantes' work: he adds a peasant wedding, a confused castle steward (broad German comic relief here), and another young knight, Don Eugenio, who tries to take liberties with Preciosa. Shortly thereafter, the farmers rush to attack the Gypsies for the sole reason that the latter, behind the disguised Don Alonzo, are unwilling to depart and leave Preciosa unprotected with Don Eugenio. As Don Eugenio is never criticized, or even accused of wrongdoing, and as ire is aroused against the Gypsies solely because they refused to yield up one of their own for his pleasure, it is apparent that traditional German anti-Gypsy feelings are much in evidence.

Moreover, the old Gypsy woman Viarda (Preciosa's "grandmother" in Cervantes' original) and the chieftain (to whom Wolff gives a greatly expanded role) are portrayed as scheming, lying, and ultimately willing to betray Preciosa, who is still part of the tribe. In Cervantes, the key to all the difficulties, the secret of Preciosa's noble birth, is provided by the merciful grandmother, both in an act of kindness for Preciosa and in order to free Andrés, who was imprisoned following a fight in which he killed a swaggering soldier who had insulted him. In Wolff's retelling, Don Alonzo is taken prisoner following the confrontation between the farmers and Gypsies. The Gypsy leaders are quite happy to leave him to his cruel fate, but Preciosa has other ideas; she vows to take her zither and sing to him in captivity:

> The beloved now to shield
> My song will raise him;
> And with softer, mild emotion,
> I will sing to him of freedom and life.
>
> Come, my close friend in suffering,
> Friend in desire and pain,
> Magic lives in your strings,
> Compassion for a loving heart.[5]

Note, here, Preciosa's antecedents. Not only does this plot draw on the same rescue-opera traditions as Beethoven's *Fidelio,* but there is also a reminiscence of the medieval legend of Richard Coeur-de-Lion and his friend, the minstrel Blondel de Nesle, who found him and sang to him of freedom when Richard was imprisoned by Emperor Henry IV. (This legend had been resuscitated by Grétry's opera of 1784, *Richard Coeur-de-lion.)* Preciosa's plan goes awry when the chieftain surprises her in the wood and tries to use force to drag her off, abandoning Don Alonzo to his fate.

It is at this point that Preciosa finds her salvation in the

form of a gun Don Alonzo had leaned against a tree. She
turns the gun on the chieftain, regains the upper hand, and
(entirely false to the spirit of Cervantes) seizes the opportunity to tell him her true feelings about the Gypsies:

> False people!
> Selfish by nature,
> Continuously operating only for profit,
> This time it's my turn.
> You yourself will lend a hand
> To free my beloved!
> Up, forward march! I'm right behind you![6]

This is, needless to say, rather unlikely talk from someone
who still thinks herself a Gypsy. By this point, things have
gone ill for the rest of the Gypsy tribe; since the confrontation
with the nobles and farmers they have been detained, and the
chieftain and Viarda now scheme to secure their release, in
the process spiriting Preciosa away from her noble lover.
After much wheedling and flattering, the perfidious Viarda
sets Alonzo up to be recaptured by his father and taken back
home. If they were to succeed, they would be rewarded with
release in the form of expulsion to Valencia, and Preciosa
would go with them.

Of course, she is saved from departure, her origins discovered, and the Gypsies are safely expelled without her. The
fact that the story ends happily, however, does not dim the
fact that in Wolff's treatment the story has become far darker
than Cervantes' had been. The Gypsy leaders are more than
willing to betray both Don Alonzo, whom they had previously taken as one of their own, and Preciosa, who *is* one of
their own. They pursue their own interest, the maintenance
of their own power, over her happiness, and the chieftain is
even willing to use violence to bend Preciosa to his will.
Clearly, these antisocial behaviors are in complete harmony

with the contemporary German view of the Gypsies as we have already seen it expressed. Notable, here, is the German race-consciousness: with Preciosa's obvious good qualities she is totally unlike the Gypsies, and she soon resents the affiliation and openly denounces them. The knight who sought to molest her escapes not only punishment but even comment; she is a mere Gypsy girl, so as a superior his right to her goes uncontested. As this briefest possible summary of a very tedious play shows, Wolff rendered Cervantes' tale thoroughly German in approach and context, with only the rough plot outlines and the Spanish locale remaining from the original, and the far more negative view of the Gypsies is clearly part of that context.

Weber's music for this play is somewhat eclectic. The chorus "Im Wald," for example, is set (appropriately enough) in traditional German *Singverein* idiom, the sort of style that the peasants and huntsmen use in *Der Freischütz* (written before but premiered after *Preciosa*). Local color of another kind appears in the form of Spanish national music; these boleros and so forth are not particularly Spanish, but simply make use of the Spanish dance rhythms. Weber reportedly researched Spanish music in preparation for the composing this work,[7] but there is Spanish presence sufficient only to provide the same kind of superficial exoticism seen in ballets: titillating in a decorous sort of way, but not profoundly exotic.

Weber described one number, the Gypsy march from Act I, as being based on a real Gypsy melody; he asserted this both in the printed score and in a letter to Wolff.[8] This march, shown in piano reduction in example 38, is not at all Spanish, but is clearly in the *style hongrois:* the melody opens with the *bókazó* rhythm, the second strain ends with a pronounced spondee in A major and lurches on in C major, and the last strain is based on syncopations and spondees. Thus, it is in

Example 38. Weber, *Preciosa*, Gypsy March from Act I.

the same Gypsy style in which he had composed the instrumental works mentioned above. The march's main theme is not the kind of Gypsy melody Weber could have found by researching Spanish music, but simply by hearing Hungarian Gypsies perform.

Dramatically, it serves to introduce the travelling Gypsies as a group. The audience hears the *style hongrois,* both in the overture and in this opening march, then is first introduced to them as a people. Despite the fact that this is the play's only number in this style, its prominent position makes the identification with the Gypsies unmistakable. By contrast, the Spanish-influenced pieces are positioned more as traditional audience diversions, buried further on in the production, and much of the other music is openly German and makes no effort to evoke anything exotic at all.

This seemingly trivial play and its one number in the *style hongrois* take on a greater significance when viewed in the light of another, more famous work. Just before composing the music for *Preciosa,* Weber finished what would become his most celebrated composition, the opera *Der Freischütz.* Even though its prevailing musical language is one of idealized German folksong, there are two numbers of a distinctly Hungarian cast. The first of these is "Hier im ird'schen Jammerthal," sung by Caspar, a hunter and marksman who has sold his soul to the devil and now seeks to bargain for three years of life in exchange for delivering up the soul of the hero, Max.

Max, through Caspar's evil offices, has just lost a shooting match to a peasant and now sits inconsolable. Caspar, hoping to win his trust, sings this short strophic song celebrating drink, women, and revelry, with the avowed purpose of cheering him up. In fact, the song is insulting; toasting Max's beloved Agathe, Caspar sings a verse in praise of cards, dice, and round-breasted maidens. As we might expect, the song projects a feeling of suppressed fury rather than revelry despite the hedonistic text. The opening of the song is given in example 39, and its materials are seen to be Hungarian: minor mode, spondee rhythms, truncated phrases, and shrill ornamentation, all of which provide a kind of subtle Gypsy backdrop for Caspar's obvious deceit and hollow celebration. This number highlights the demonic aspects of Caspar's

Example 39. Weber, *Der Freischütz*, Act I, Caspar's song, "Hier im ird'schen Jammerthal," opening.

character, polarizing him and Max by using an entirely different musical language with its own dark and threatening associations.[9] The song is more an allusion than a full-blown Hungarian essay, so the musical references must operate on an almost subliminal level. Weber's audience would have been reminded of Gypsy associations, not the Gypsies themselves.

Interestingly, this is the first number of the opera in which a character sings—loudly, protesting too much—something he does not mean at all. Caspar's real motivation is fear for his fate and rage at his circumstances. His *modus operandi* consists of lies and schemes, and he has no real loyalties; in all of this he is the exact opposite of Max. But scheming, falsehood, contemptuous pride, and professed rejoicing while one is really in a ongoing state of damnation, both here and in the world to come, are all inherent in the Gypsy stereotype. Caspar is no Gypsy, of course; they do not appear in this opera. But when he dissembles, when his situation resembles that of the Gypsies, his music reflects theirs also. It is a deft compositional stroke.

There is a second *style hongrois* number in this opera. Ännchen's romanze from Act III, "Einst träumte meiner sel'gen Base," makes clear use of the same idiom. This number, somewhat dramatically disadvantaged in that it was inserted at the request of the singer and is poorly assimilated into the operatic whole, has Ännchen, best friend of Max's fiancée Agathe, trying to distract her friend from evil dreams and presentiments. To this end, she tells her a short, idiotic story about a relation beset by evil visions, which turns out to be caused by nothing more threatening than the watchdog. Example 40 gives the opening.

Several familiar features are immediately apparent. There is a rhapsodic solo flourish (on viola, not violin, but the style is certainly the same) that scampers up and down two octaves. The accompaniment, which remains unchanged throughout, is a string tremolo that, when combined with the solo, suggests whispering cimbaloms. The key is G minor, and on top of this shimmering, minor texture Ännchen sings a flirtatious, *Zingarese*-type melody in predominantly dotted

Example 40. Weber, *Der Freischütz*, Act III, Ännchen's song, "Einst träumte meiner sel'gen Base," opening.

rhythms, suggestive of *verbunkos*. Moreover, the text hints at dream divination, an old Gypsy tradition, and Ännchen, too, is dissembling and nervously masking her true feelings.

An argument for Weber's informed use of the *style hongrois* certainly cannot be based on this hastily added trifle; it must and does hinge on Caspar and *Preciosa*. On the other hand, it is undeniable that Ännchen's *romanze* uses this vernacular and that her mood is equivocal at the time she sings it. What is clear is that in *Preciosa* and *Der Freischütz* this musical dialect is not appearing either at random or as an elegant, "characteristic" diversion. It appears in specific contexts and as a clearly alternative musical language, set off in contrast to the music around it.

Weber's use of this style represents a profound development because, as far as can be established, he is the first composer who used it to suggest not only Hungarian Gypsies but especially aspects of their stereotype and situation. This is not surprising; as an agile, multifaceted composer of dramatic music, he would be ideally situated to blend musical languages, cultural associations, and plot considerations together in this new way and to be well understood in doing so. Indeed, the composer Louis Spohr, having abandoned his own *Freischütz* project on learning of Weber's opera, felt that Weber's talent for writing for the general masses (read: communicating with the mob) was the only way to explain the work's success.

Weber's individual deployment of the *style hongrois* did not go unnoticed in the compositional community. A friend of his, an admirer of *Der Freschütz* and one of the greatest composers of the nineteenth century, seems to have had a penetrating understanding of the dialect's possibilities as Weber demonstrated them in the instrumental works, literally in *Preciosa,* and more subtly in *Der Freischütz*. Further, he would eventually come to use the *style hongrois* with even greater deftness and command, and with far deeper resonances in his own life.

CHAPTER 7

Schubert

I

FRANZ SCHUBERT was a devotee, although not an unquestioning one, of Weber and his music. Superficial similarities between the two composers are easy to identify: commitment to song, sympathy for vernacular styles, and attraction to the Romantic aesthetic and forms of expression, to name only three. Schubert and Weber had been friends in Vienna in 1821–22 and spent a considerable amount of time together,[1] and Schubert is known to have been particularly enamored of *Der Freischütz*. As his friend Josef von Spaun later related,

> Schubert was a great admirer of Carl Maria [von] Weber and he liked *Der Freischütz* immensely. He was absolutely delighted with the men's quintet in the first act, in which the unlucky marksman is comforted, and maintained that there were few more beautiful compositions.[2]

149

Schubert also hoped that Weber could provide professional help. The two were in communication about Schubert's opera *Alfonso und Estrella,* and in the fall of 1822 he received a letter from Weber he described as "very promising,"[3] although it amounted to nothing in the end. A strong tradition suggests that, ironically, it was Schubert's affection for *Der Freischütz* that poisoned their friendship; he did not feel Weber's *Euryanthe* measured up to the earlier work, and when Weber requested his opinion he gave this opinion frankly. As the story goes, the elder composer, taking offense, took no further action on Schubert's behalf, thus dealing his professional aspirations another heavy blow.

There is a fair amount of corroboration from sources intimate with the principals: Spaun, Weber's son Max Maria (although he would have been an infant at the time), and Helmina von Chézy (librettist to both Schubert and Weber) recount close variants of this story.[4] What is certain is that Schubert was not pleased with *Euryanthe.* On November 30, 1823, he wrote to Franz Schober, a greatly admired friend and self-styled aesthete, that "Weber's *Euryanthe* turned out wretchedly and its bad reputation was quite justified in my opinion."[5] Otto Erich Deutsch has pointed out, however, that later meetings between the two composers do not harmonize with the anecdote as it stands and that for all its color the tale is probably grossly exaggerated.[6]

What is important for our purposes is that Schubert knew and admired Weber in general and *Der Freischütz* in particular. It is very likely that Weber's deployment of the *style hongrois* in that work, his use of it to lend a situation or text deeper significance through reference to the Gypsies, was not lost on Schubert. Indeed, he may have used it as a model, as can be seen in the second half of *Winterreise.*

This famous song cycle, set to poems by Wilhelm Müller, has a sentimental, pathos-laden plot ideal for Schubert's compositional imagination and perfect for the spirit of the time. The young, unremittingly grief-stricken poet-narrator bids his lover farewell, as it has become painfully obvious that she is no longer his. He wanders city and country, wallowing in misery and gravitating toward madness, until his endless, comfortless journey concludes in a meeting with a battered and downtrodden hurdy-gurdy player. This serves as both end and beginning, as he must decide to remain with the old man, to travel, or to disappear into oblivion.

Three of these songs have a Hungarian-Gypsy character, and as with Weber the subject matter in each case reflects an aspect of the Gypsy stereotype. The first example is the twentieth song, *Der Wegweiser* (The Guidepost), which deals with the poet's avoidance of other people, his desire for rest, his destiny as a wanderer, and so on. Some of the text runs as follows:

> Why do I avoid the highways
> travelled by other wanderers,
> and search out hidden paths
> through snowbound rocky heights?
>
> I have done nothing
> to make me avoid people.
>
> I trudge ceaselessly on,
> seeking rest, and finding none.
>
> I must travel a road
> by which no one has ever returned.[7]

The parallel with the Gypsies needs little explanation: exclusion from society and a destiny of aimless, miserable wandering are obvious associations. The first verse of this song is seen in example 41; immediately apparent is both its prevailing minor mode and the weary, plodding gait that will become very familiar in Schubert's instrumental *style hongrois* works. On the local level, m. 12 and m. 14 have clear *bókazó*

Example 41. Schubert, *Der Wegweiser*, mm. 6–20.

rhythms in the left hand, and in mm. 16–20 the piano and voice alternate a dotted rhythm figure reminiscent of *verbunkos*.

As with the pieces from *Der Freischütz*, the stylistic deployment is circumspect, not literal; the suggestions of alienation and a bleak, wandering destiny in this song call for a music with a subtle Gypsy inflection, not excess. The *style hongrois* speaks a bit more freely in song number 22, *Muth* (Courage). The text, in its entirety, runs as follows:

> If snow flies in my face,
> I brush it off.
> If my heart speaks within me
> I sing brightly and cheerfully.
>
> I do not hear what it is saying to me;
> I have no ears.
> I do not feel the cause of its complaint—
> complaining is for fools.
>
> Gaily forth into the world,
> in spite of wind and weather!
> If there be no god on earth.
> then we ourselves are gods![8]

This song is a close relative of Caspar's song of rage, defiance, and false revelry from *Der Freischütz*. Example 42 gives two excerpts from *Muth;* the first shows the minor mode, prominent spondees, and lopsided 3 + 2 vocal phrasing. The second shows, on the repetition of the line "merrily into the world despite wind and weather," an explosive, unprepared leap to the relative major. The effect can be hair-raising: the song has remained to this point in the tonality of A, flickering between major and minor modes, and it is as if the poet's irrational rage and self-contempt suddenly catapult the harmony a third away. From C major, Schubert immediately jerks back to A major via the dominant, and the song ends in A minor. These gestures evoke the nonfunctional harmonic practices associated with Gypsy musicians.

Example 42. Schubert, *Muth.*

42a. Mm. 1–11.

By this point in the cycle, we know the depths of the poet's torment, and just two songs ago he was bleakly complaining of wandering snowbound, rocky heights. As he pretends to make light of his situation, we know him to be either dissembling or mad; the music, very angular, mercurial, and Gypsy-like, tells us he is dissembling.

The last song of the cycle, *Der Leiermann,* is the most obvious example of the *style hongrois.* Here is the poem:

> Over beyond the village
> stands a hurdy-gurdy man,
> and with his numb fingers
> he grinds as best he can.

Lu - stig in die Welt hin - ein ge - gen Wind und

Wet - ter!

42b. Mm. 31–36.

Barefoot on the ice,
he moves to and fro,
and his little tray
is always empty.

Nobody cares to hear him,
nobody looks at him;
and the dogs snarl
around the old man.

And he lets everything go
as it will;
he grinds, and his hurdy-gurdy
is never silent.

Queer old man,
shall I go with you?
Will you grind out my songs
on your hurdy-gurdy?[9]

The relationship to Gypsydom is obvious: the poet has found another outcast, a musician ostracized to the point that his money tray is always empty and even the dogs snarl at him. Taking no notice, he cares only for his musical instrument, which is never silent; indeed, he seemingly depends on his music to survive. The hurdy-gurdy is an interesting choice of instrument here: originally, the hurdy-gurdy's use was closely related to that of the bagpipe, particularly when used as part of a duo before the era of the Gypsy bands. Indeed, Sárosi says that even in recent times recordings could be made of peasants playing in traditional hurdy-gurdy and clarinet duos. As he put it, "the hurdy-gurdy, though a stringed instrument, shows a strong resemblance to the bagpipes in sound and in its use among the people."[10] The hurdy-gurdy per se was not usually associated with the Gypsies, but it is appropriate here because of context and similarity to the bagpipe, which Gypsies were known to play. It seems clear that Schubert was using some initiative in going beyond the literal text of Müller's poem (the hurdy-gurdy was his choice, after all, and not Schubert's) to draw the Gypsy parallel by giving the music an unmistakably Hungarian cast, one of almost Bartókian faithfulness.

Two excerpts from *Der Leiermann* are shown in example 43. Of course, the most obvious characteristic is the hurdy-gurdy's drone; this bass fifth will continue unchanged throughout the song. The tonality is minor, and the melody is of limited range and repeats in circular fashion. The drone continues to sound even when it clashes with the dominant harmony in mm. 4–5 and 7–8, and mm. 9–10 show that the opening vocal melody hints at the *Kuruc*-fourth. The excerpt in 43b is even more obvious: the instrumental melody in m. 49 stresses the augmented second between F and G-sharp and then descends to the cadence figure through a series of crying Hungarian sixths in m. 50. Measure 53, on the words "Wunderlicher Alter," outlines a *Kuruc*-fourth in a clear and unmis-

Example 43. Schubert, *Der Leiermann.*

43a. Mm. 1–10.

takable way, rather like example 35a, from Liszt's *Drei Zigeuner,* shown in chapter 5.

II

To my knowledge, no one has noticed the overtly Hungarian
aspects of these three songs, or the way Schubert used the

43*b*. Mm. 49–53.

style hongrois to signify the extramusical ideas outlined above. In fact, Gypsy influence of any kind in Schubert's music is discussed only in the most obvious cases, and then only grudgingly. This is where we begin to encounter the critical discomfort with this music.

One example among many negative responses to Schubert's use of this idiom is provided by J. A. Westrup, in his discussion of the Quintet in C Major for Strings, D. 956. Every movement of that work contains at least one pronounced section or passage in the *style hongrois,* but Westrup notices it only in the finale, a spirited Hungarian dancing-song that was shown in example 30:

> We might have wished that the Quintet should end otherwise, that the finale should capture the lofty tone of the first movement. We may not want to be reminded of the open-air cafe and the Hungarian band. But Schubert saw no reason to segregate music into compartments—and Brahms agreed with him. We must either frankly accept his view or confess a disappointment.[11]

He is even clearer further on:

> The influence of the café and the theatre is everywhere. Its presence is not necessarily disconcerting. It is only when it is obviously at war with its context that

we feel a sense of embarrassment. To dismiss these
incongruities is no compliment to Schubert. . . . Better
the String Quintet with its uncomfortable finale than
no quintet at all.[12]

Westrup's discontent is palpable. His allusions to disap-
pointment, music appropriate to "the open-air café," and
above all the "uncomfortable" finale's lack of loftiness make
painfully clear just how he rates such music. This type of
response shows a profound discomfort with a music that has
retained its popular, light-entertainment associations despite
its assimilation into the concert repertoire.

Schubert's *Divertissement à l'Hongroise* D. 818 (completed in
fall, 1824), the four-hand piano piece that furnished several of
the examples in chapter 5, is his only work to acknowledge
its Hungarian-Gypsy idiom in the title. As his most substantial and extended essay in that style, it is every bit the
catalogue of Gypsy performance gestures and inflections that
Liszt's Hungarian Rhapsodies and Brahm's Hungarian
Dances would later be, but it still provokes more condescension than serious discussion among Schubert scholars. His
own contemporaries, however, spoke very highly of it, and
Liszt liked it enough to transcribe the whole for piano solo in
1846. Schubert's friend Karl von Schönstein referred to it as
"one of the grandest of his pianoforte pieces,"[13] and Spaun
called it "his beautiful *Divertissement à l'Hongroise.*"[14]

Without looking too closely, it has generally been assumed
that this work is the first appearance of the *style hongrois* in
Schubert's works. The traditional explanation stems from his
friends and contemporaries and attributes his use of this style
to a lengthy stay in Hungary through summer and fall of
1824, at which time he was staying at the Esterházy home at
Zseliz and was engaged as music master to the prince's two
daughters. Anselm Hüttenbrenner, for example, said that
Schubert collected material for the *Divertissement* while stay-

ing in Hungary and that Gypsy music had interested him a great deal;[15] Karl von Schönstein's account had Schubert basing the *Divertissement* on a bewitching song sung by a Hungarian kitchen maid, whom he had overheard.[16]

These reminiscences may well be true in their particulars, but the impression they create, that Schubert had not encountered Gypsy music before that trip to Hungary, most certainly is not. For one thing, he had stayed at Esterháza before, in 1818, but to judge from his work he retained little or nothing of Hungarian-Gypsy music from that first trip. Furthermore, the *Divertissement* is at least the fifth work utilizing the *style hongrois,* not the first: the F minor *Moment Musical* (D. 780, op. 94/3), and the final movements of the A minor string quartet (D. 804), the Octet (D. 803), and the four-hand Sonata in C Major (also known as the *Grand Duo,* D. 812) all predate the *Divertissement* and possess a strong Hungarian-Gypsy character. At least the *Moment,* the quartet, and Octet were completed long before he left Vienna. (For a chronological list of Schubert's works using the *style hongrois,* see the Appendix.)

In any case, as we have already seen, Schubert would not have had to have gone to Hungary to hear Gypsy music; Gypsy musicians were well established in Vienna by this time, and the *style hongrois* had already been used by Mozart, Haydn, Beethoven, Hummel, and Weber. The domestic *verbunkos* publications, too, had already been appearing for forty years at the time the *Divertissement* was composed. In 1814 Schubert himself arranged the composer Matiegka's guitar trio for guitar quartet, and the work features a "*Zingara*" (Gypsy) movement that uses an actual *verbunkos* melody.[17] Not only had he heard the style, then, he had firsthand working knowledge of it. Both its absence from his works before 1823 and its sudden appearance at that time are surprising, particularly considering the fluent and eloquent way in which he (seemingly immediately) was able to use it.

Schubert's use of the *style hongrois* both as an attractive and accessible musical language and also as representative of a large complex of extramusical ideas followed Weber's lead. It also took the process to a much higher level. Superficially, this was an "exotic" and increasingly popular style that had proven commercial appeal. But in using it, Schubert was identifying on a deeper level with the propagators of the style, the Hungarian Gypsies, whose mistreatment, ostracism, defiance, and reputed reliance upon music as the expression of their sorrows had resonances in his own life.

III

Schubert's relationship to Viennese society at large was an odd one in that while he is often considered quintessentially Viennese, he lived in clear and conscious separation from the wider Viennese society. The letters and diary entries of Schubert and his intimates present a clear picture of both his alienation and emotional reliance on a close group of sympathetic, artistically inclined friends. His general circumstances provided ample need for that kind of support: wide acceptance of his music remained elusive (despite some critical approval), the securing of an official position would have necessitated currying favor, for which he had no taste, and his material circumstances were usually precarious. From a relatively early age, Schubert asserted fierce independence from prescribed patterns: he openly renounced marriage, proudly and repeatedly disavowed social norms and their attendant family responsibilities, and held those who blindly conformed in contempt. Withal, he seems to have maintained a good humor and optimism about things, but only until one critical point.

From the time he contracted syphilis in late 1822, a mood of profound distress becomes apparent. His writings document a prevailing depression and a yearning for release. By the beginning of 1823 he had to leave his lodgings in Schober's home and move back in with his family;[18] and the entire convalescence from the initial cataclysmic phase of the disease lasted at least until late autumn of 1824. At the earliest stages of the disease his writings are very infrequent, and as it progressed his outlook took on an increasingly dark character, and the references to freedom became more wistful, imploring, and in a sense hopeless.

His first *style hongrois* work, the F minor *Moment Musical* (D. 780, op. 94/3), dates from some time in the dismal year of 1823; in December it appeared in a musical journal. Example 44 gives two excerpts: the opening theme (44a), which features a close relative of the *bókazó* rhythm and prominent spondees, and another segment (44b) showing spondees, a syncopated accompaniment figure, and parallel sixths. This miniature appears in isolation, and no information concerning the immediate circumstances of its composition or the sudden adoption of the new musical language survives. What is curious is the extent to which it looks like a compositional study, or experiment: while it is clearly evocative of the Hungarian-Gypsy ethos, the piece does not venture into the emotional extremes generally associated with it. The mood is relatively restrained throughout, with brief mercurial flashes here and there, and the Gypsy gestures are used in a careful, controlled fashion. His later *style hongrois* works would have far greater scope and range. This seems like a very competent, beautiful, but somehow not wholly assured exercise in a new language.

One possible stimulus for Schubert to begin exploring the possibilities of the *style hongrois* might have occurred in July, 1823, when he was already quite ill, but perhaps no longer

Example 44. Schubert, Moment Musical in F Minor, D. 780, op. 94/3.

44a. Mm. 2–5.

44b. Mm. 19–26.

housebound. On the fifth of that month, Wolff's *Preciosa*, with Weber's music, was performed at the Theater an der Wien, where Schubert's own *Rosamunde* would be put on six months later.[19] Of course, *Preciosa* is only one very obvious juxtaposition of the *style hongrois* and the German stereotype of the Gypsies, but we know that Schubert was already familiar with *Der Freischütz*, and the *Winterreise* songs (written later, in autumn, 1827) suggest that he followed Weber's associative deployment of the Gypsy idiom. The Vienna performance of *Preciosa* occurred roughly in the middle of the period during which the F minor *Moment Musical* was composed, and at this time Schubert's health would have put him in a vulnerable, and perhaps impressionable, frame of mind. Of course, in the absence of any further evidence this single point must remain purely speculative.

The writings of his circle provide ample testimony about his emotional state during his illness. On February 13, 1824, Moritz von Schwind, a friend who later achieved fame as a painter, wrote to Schober with some transitory good news: "Schubert now keeps a fortnight's fast and confinement. He looks much better and is very bright, very comically hungry and writes quartets and German Dances and variations without number."[20] One of the quartets was the A minor (D. 804), finished in March; the opening of its finale, shown in example 45, shows characteristic spondee rhythms, accented anapests, and asymmetrical phrases (5 + 4). The Octet (D. 803) dates from the same time and also shows pronounced Hungarianisms in the final movement: irregular phrasing in the main theme, Gypsy violin flourishes and cimbalom imitations (the violin and cimbalom gestures are shown in example 46, the *Andante molto* section). The clear and substantial use of the *style hongrois* in both the quartet and the Octet, after using the style only in a decade-old arrangement and a somewhat tentative miniature the previous year, suggests that the realization of its relevance and expressive possibilities was for him a sudden one.

The bright mood to which Schwind refers, however, was unfortunately neither permanent nor even dominant. Schubert's general feeling at the time seems to have remained grim, as a well-known letter poignantly illustrates. On March 31, 1824 he wrote to Leopold Kupelwieser, a friend and artist touring Italy:

> In a word, I feel myself to be the most unhappy and wretched creature in the world. Imagine a man whose health will never be right again, and who in sheer despair over this ever makes things worse and worse,

Example 45. Schubert, String Quartet in A Minor, D. 804, IV, mm. 1–20.

instead of better; imagine a man, I say, whose most brilliant hopes have perished, to whom the felicity of love and friendship have nothing to offer but pain. . . . I ask you, is he not a miserable, unhappy being? . . . Each night, on retiring to bed, I hope I may not wake again,

Example 46. Schubert, Octet, D. 803, final movement, mm. 370–72.

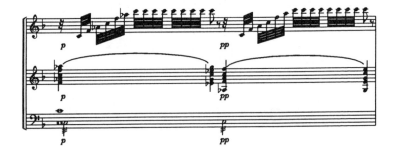

> and each morning but recalls yesterday's grief. Thus,
> joyless and friendless, I should pass my days, did not
> Schwind visit me now and again and turn on me a ray
> of those sweet days of the past.[21]

Other letters from Schubert and his circle document that his health and recovery (and, correspondingly, his mood) had been up and down in the months preceding this letter and the quartet. But a few weeks after the "comical" hunger and furious composing mentioned by Schwind, Schubert had reverted to "the most unhappy and wretched creature in the world."

Like others of his circle who contracted this disease and suffered lengthy convalescences, Schubert left Vienna for an extended period.[22] This was the summer (1824) of his second sojourn in Zseliz at the Esterházy estate to serve as music master. He departed on May 25, but his letters indicate that he remained unhappy throughout the summer despite the agreeability of the countryside, the physically restorative nature of his stay, and considerable compositional fruitfulness. A letter to Schober of September 21 complains,

> If only we were together, you, Schwind, Kuppel, and I, any misfortune would seem to me but a trivial matter; but here we are, separated, each in a different corner, and that is what makes me unhappy. I want to exclaim with Goethe: "Who will bring back one hour of that sweet time?" . . . Now I set here alone in the depths of the Hungarian country whither I unfortunately let myself be enticed a second time without having a single person with whom I could speak a sensible word.[23]

It is during this unhappy stay in Zseliz that Schubert began composing the *Divertissement,* his most thoroughgoing essay in the *style hongrois.* This title may fairly be seen as something of a compromise. Schubert wrote far lighter, more "diversionlike" music than this, including such strongly Hungarian-tinged pieces as the aforementioned *Moment Musical* and the *Impromptus* op. 90/2 in E-flat major and 142/4 in F minor. The *Divertissement* is a monumental three-movement work, and has a prevailing darkness of mood that suggests a prodigious but troubled creativity. On the other hand, music drawing this heavily on a popular style might predictably be called "Diversion," particularly when its unique formal structure precludes the title "sonata." For this piece, the title *Divertissement* is an almost ironic understatement for the effect produced by the moodiness of the consistent *style hongrois* and its cultural associations.

Schubert's next Hungarian-influenced work is the *Andante* of the "Great" C major symphony (already seen in example 21), composed in the summer of 1825.[24] Following an unhealthy and unproductive period in the months preceding April, Schubert went on tour with a friend, the singer Vogl. The trip represented a physical, social, and musical liberation for him, and his description of their music making indicates the kind of exultation he was taking in musical activities on the road: "The manner in which Vogl sings and the way I accompany, as though we were one at such a moment, is something quite new and unheard-of for these people."[25] Another letter describes a full six weeks spent "quite agreeably" in Gmunden with Vogl.[26]

This *Andante* and the D major piano sonata, which dates from September of that year and also contains some marked Gypsy elements, mark the only happy period in Schubert's life that saw him utilize the *style hongrois*. More than mere good spirits, though, his life consisted of carefree travelling, ideal music making, the constant companionship of a trusted friend, and above all blessed relief from a lengthy period of illness and hopelessness. Schubert and Vogl, in their freely wandering leisure, became obvious analogues to those who lived their lives on the road, thus suggesting a musical reference.[27]

The period between his idyllic trip with Vogl in the summer of 1825 and the fall of 1827 seems to have been a rather contented time for Schubert, and predictably enough no *style hongrois* pieces were composed. His serenity and inactivity are well documented. In the diary of Edward Bauernfeld, dramatist and close friend of the composer, there is this unconsciously ironic entry of March 8, 1826: "Schubert has the right mixture of the idealist and the realist. The world seems fair to him."[28] A letter of Schubert's from late May, 1826, has this isolated remark: "I am not working at all."[29] And on July 10, he writes to Bauernfeld, "I have no money at all, and altogether things go very badly with me. I do not trouble about it, and am cheerful."[30] Clearly, at this time the

composer was not feeling particularly alienated from anything, or under much pressure of any sort. In the fall of 1827,
however, his mood began to darken again, and his health
took a turn for the worse.

The gathering clouds can be detected in his letters. A letter
of September 27 laments,

> Already it becomes clear to me that I was only too
> happy at Graz, and I cannot as yet get accustomed to
> Vienna. True, it is rather large, but then it is empty of
> cordiality, candor, genuine thought, reasonable words,
> and especially of intelligent deeds. There is so much
> confused chatter that one hardly knows whether one is
> on one's head or one's heels, and one rarely or never
> achieves any inward contentment.[31]

To the same friend he writes on October 12, "I hope that
your honour is in better health than I, for my usual headaches
are already assailing me again."[32] In a letter of October 15, he
described himself as "utterly unfit for any society."[33]

It is at this time that the *style hongrois* reappears in his
works; pieces featuring it, moreover, appear in greater con-
centration. The three *Winterreise* songs already discussed date
from this time. So, too, do the Impromptus to which I
alluded above: opus 90/2 in E-flat major, an attractive salon
piece with an explosive Gypsy middle section in B minor,
dates from summer-fall, and op. 142/4 (an F-minor dancing-
song) from September. In December, Schubert composed
the Fantasy for violin and piano in C major, which opens
with a stylized Gypsy improvisation: soloistic violin roulades
are accompanied by cimbalomlike tremolos in the piano (see
example 47).

Schubert's final year was, despite his ruined health, extremely productive, and two of the most celebrated works
from that time have clear Hungarian-Gypsy content. The
year 1828 began with the *Fantasia* in F minor for piano, four-

Example 47. Schubert, *Fantasie* in C Major for violin and piano, D. 934, mm. 5–10.

hands. In addition to having the same relentless and fatalistic gait as *Der Wegweiser* and the *Andante* of the "Great," its opening melody is based on the *Kuruc*-fourth, as was shown in example 35c. There followed in September the String Quintet in C Major (the work to whose finale Westrup objected), an unqualified masterpiece that also coincided with a period of renewed ill health. According to his brother Ferdinand, "In September already Schubert ailed and doctored. However, his indisposition again decreased somewhat."[34] Following a short pleasure trip, he suddenly took ill, and this proved to be the final time.

IV

The temporal correlation between Schubert's *style hongrois* pieces and his blackest emotional periods is clearly too close to be dismissed as coincidental. Except for the two pieces from the brief, liberating *Wandersommer* of 1825, these works were engendered by his emotional low points. His contemporaneous writings speak of health forever lost, of irretrievable hope, and of joylessness, friendlessness, and loneliness precisely at those times in which the *style hongrois* appears in his work.

The precise causes of his depression cannot definitively be identified, nor need they be; there were myriad possibilities. In addition to the obvious health concerns, throughout this period Schubert's operatic aspirations suffered setback after setback, amounting to increasing frustration in an area in which he had spent considerable time and effort. Still, he continued to try to get works produced and did not refer to the periodic defeats in the same morbid tone as he did his health and mood.

Material circumstances, after all, continued to be precarious for him, a situation that would wear anyone's favorable outlook thin. Of course, we also saw that at other times he could keep his mood independent from this kind of care. On the personal side, he had close friends but, as a bachelor, no family life of his own, and his relationship with his father continued to be problematic. Familial emotional support was provided only by his siblings.

One strong possibility is that in his use of the *style hongrois,* Schubert could well have been making the same connection we saw made by Théophile Gautier (see the conclusion to chapter 4). The Rom, maintaining a freedom-loving lifestyle in the face of societal disapproval and abuse, represented an obvious analogy to the composer and musician, battling poverty and societal neglect at every turn but clinging tenaciously to the unconstrained artistic life and pursuit of the beautiful. The use of Hungarian-Gypsy music would have thus enabled him to make a powerful personal statement regarding his own situation, encoding his meaning in musical language rather than mere words.

Another very plausible explanation for Schubert's use of this language pertains to his personal life. Maynard Solomon's compellingly argued and meticulously documented article, "Franz Schubert and the Peacocks of Benvenuto Cellini," suggests that Schubert was a homosexual, and that for this reason he felt impelled to separate himself from the greater Viennese society and to take refuge in a smaller circle of like-minded artistic friends. It is apparent that this separation was not a completely satisfactory solution because, despite emotional support and intimate friendship, his writings return with frequency and bitterness to societal conformity, and his refusal and resentment of it, and to squabbles within the circle itself. The idea to which he returns again and again is freedom: freedom from care and rejection, and freedom to follow one's own path, make one's own decisions, and follow one's own motivations. Given the cultural climate and Weber's example, it seems no great speculation to suggest that Schubert gave voice to these feelings with the musical language and gestures of the Gypsies, a people who (like homosexuals) were held to value freedom above all, who were wrongfully accused of every imaginable vice and moral failing, who nonetheless lived resolutely in defiance of established mores, and who were regularly made to suffer for it.[35]

Understanding the Gypsies' position in society, we are now in a position to answer Westrup's objections to the juxtaposition of pathos and the "light" Gypsy music in the Schubert String Quintet. It was not the light, casual gaiety of a Gypsy band that Schubert was evoking; it was the desperate, tragic reveling of the Gypsy outcast paid to provide merriment in the teeth of his own sorrow. Musical reference was being made to the dark inner world of these cafe musicians: those who, it was imagined, expressed their deep and unnamable grief with music of both profound pathos and furious abandon.

Given all of this, one assumption now seems untenable. The traditional idea that Schubert's pieces in the *style hongrois* are merely light, popular, occasional, or even trivial ignores his knowledge of Weber, his undoubted awareness of contemporary Gypsy stereotypes, and the fact that he composed these pieces when he was the least suited emotionally to write harmless occasional music. Rather, the reverse of that assumption turns out to be the least speculative of all: at his points of lowest psychological ebb, bereft of physical health and emotional support, Schubert's inspiration found voice in the music of a group whose abominable circumstances must have presented an irresistible parallel to his own.

CHAPTER 8

Liszt

I

TO JUDGE from the musical record, Liszt was one of Schubert's greatest admirers. He edited and reworked a number of Schubert's works, the best known being the song transcriptions and an arrangement of the *Wanderer Fantasy* for piano and orchestra. He was also sufficiently enamored of Schubert's *style hongrois* pieces to edit or transcribe at least three of them: the F minor *Moment Musical,* the *Impromptu,* op. 90/2, and the *Divertissement à l'Hongroise.*

Very surprising, given this proof of his interest, is the following excerpt from his expansive book, *Des Bohémiens et de leur musique en Hongrie* (1859),[1] later Englished as *The Gipsy in Music:*

> During a stay which Schubert made at the chateau of one of the first families of Hungary he transcribed some Bohemian motives for the piano, forming them into a piece for four hands, one of the most ravishing of all his works, and entitled "Divertissement Hongrois [*sic*]."

In examining it, however, it is easy to perceive that he did not look upon these productions as exotic plants; samples revealing the flora of a zone as yet unexplored. He did not give himself the trouble to penetrate sufficiently its spirit and intimate sense.

He seemed, for instance, to regard an abrupt modulation as *lapsus linguae,* intentional repetitions as pleonasm; strange chords as barbarisms; and all unusual augmentations and diminutions as incorrect—all of these being features which constitute the Bohemian style. He concerned himself only with the broad design and with the motives displayed by the melodic progressions; making himself familiar also with the special function taken over by the rhythms in its several changes, but not troubling overmuch about any importance which might attach to the ornamentation. It is, in short, quite evident, from the manner in which he treated Bohemian motives, that he did not recognise them as belonging to an art different from every other; constructed on another foundation and built on different principles. He estimated the fragments which reached him to be mere off-shoots, disfigured and disseminated haphazard by coarse, rough players; and fondly imagined he was giving them some value by trimming them up according to our rules and methods.

Probably he may have even thought he was doing them quite sufficient justice and honour by rescuing those which seemed to lend themselves best to his purpose from complete oblivion—that purpose being to send them out in a precious setting to be recognised as from the hands of the master. . . .

The idea never so much as occurred to him that he was in the presence of a great movement; with regard to which the question was not one of restoring or arranging, but of seizing the style, and reconstructing the marvellous ensemble, by intuitive divination of the proportion occupied by details and the immense part played by them.[2]

Entirely apart from the prose style, many questions are raised by this puzzling passage. There is no shortage of abrupt modulations, brusque harmonic shifts, or "strange chords" throughout Schubert's work. Literal repetitions are present in such measure that even the Viennese pianists Paul Badura-Skoda and Jorg Demus omit some in their recording of the work; it is hard to imagine where Shubert might have found them redundant. Liszt's entire criticism is basically unsupported by the music, but worst is the suggestion that Schubert somehow failed to recognize the essential differences between the standard musical language and the *style hongrois*. Schubert "spoke" this vernacular as well as any composer in history, and the *Divertissement* is as evocative and compelling a piece as any of the Gypsy essays by Brahms or Liszt himself. It is therefore tempting to conclude that the author of the above passage had no real familiarity with Schubert's work, which Liszt, as transcriber and arranger, had. As will be seen below, the issue of authorship is by no means as simple as the single name on the title page would suggest.

This book is obviously problematic, but as we saw in chapter 5 it also contains some valuable material, and as the only such source associated with the *style hongrois* it requires examination. Originally intended to be a kind of prolegomenon to the *Rhapsodies hongroises* (Hungarian Rhapsodies), most of which appeared in 1851 and 1853, it eventually reached book length and was published six years later. Liszt's original premise was that music so exotic and characteristic needed an explanation when put before the public. This is an interesting position: in taking it he seems not to acknowledge the possibility that the Rhapsodies might not prove unfathomable. After all, Europe had already seen seventy-five years or so of the *style hongrois,* and he himself had already published, in the 1840s, a good portion of the Rhapsodies' raw material as the *Ungarische Nationalmelodien*. Moreover, "Gypsy" music had received a boost from the failed Hungarian revolution of 1848, which forced many people to move west and raised the public consciousness about things Hungarian. All this notwithstanding, he offered this work as both an explanation for the *Rhapsodies hongroises,* and as a discussion of the Gypsies themselves, their music, and their musical role in Hungary.

The book's central premise is the first major problem. Liszt proceeded from the assumption that the music from which the *style hongrois* evolved was a Gypsy creation and that the Hungarians merely supported and enjoyed it. The Hungarians might have found this mistake to be more forgivable from a less ambitious writer, or a non-Hungarian, but from an originally Hungarian cosmopolite it was felt to be a grave offense.

The very real dependence of Hungarian musical culture on the Gypsies only made the error harder to stomach. Hungarians had indeed long left the cultivation of their own popular-art music to the Gypsies, and admitted so, although not always graciously. One journalistic reaction to Liszt's book asserts precisely this, saying, "we thought . . . that the music is Hungarian whereas its principal guardian is the gypsy," adding fussily, "although this is not always to its advantage."[3] Gabor Mátray, nineteenth-century scholar, librarian, and founder of Hungarian musicology, wrote the following five years before Liszt's book first appeared,

> Unfortunately earlier the more cultured Hungarian did not generally practice the national music, and entrusted its preservation and spreading only to gypsies; on account of which it must not be a matter of surprise if foreign musicians begin to doubt the true Hungarian character of the national music customarily performed by our gypsies, and if they regard this as being Indian gypsy music rather than Hungarian music.[4]

Thus, the problem was not the acknowledgment of the Gypsies' importance as custodians of the performance tradition; that was indisputable. Liszt, however, ascribed the actual creation of such music to the Gypsies, in the following poetic genesis story:

> In the very act of passing the bow across the violin-strings a natural inspiration suggested itself; and, without any search for them, there came rhythms, cadences, modulations, melodies and tonal discourses. . . . In his music [the Gypsy] revealed that golden ray of interior light proper to himself, which otherwise the world would never have known or suspected. He made it dance and glitter in the fascination of a wild harmony, fantastic and full of discords; and thus, by a mixture of unexpected outline, glaring colour, sudden change and quick transformation, endowed it with its many seductive features.[5]

Such phrases as "which otherwise the world would never have known or suspected" undoubtedly were found treasonous by the Hungarians. Even when he tries to give Hungary its due, Liszt took refuge in hollow prolixity. Note that for all the talk of rhythm he does not acknowledge the origin of many typical Gypsy rhythms in the Hungarian language:

> The Bohemian art can never be separated from Hungary, whose arms it must for ever bear on seal and banner. To Hungary it owes a life passed entirely within its limits and in its atmosphere. To Hungary also the attainment of its virility and maturity are due; dependent as these were upon appreciation of its noble elements. It has also Hungary to thank for supply of its greatest needs—comprehension and sympathy. The haughtiness of its rhythms, their imposing dignity and sudden cries, remindful of those of a startled courser at sound of the trumpet—all from the very first, went straight to the Hungarian heart.[6]

Hungary only understood the rhythms, in Liszt's view—it did not produce them. The "haughtiness" of the rhythms was apparently a Gypsy property. Further, the earnest acknowledgments of the gratitude owed Hungary by the Bohemian art have a naïveté bordering on the weird; not only was the music Hungarian to begin with, but the Gypsies' circumstances in that country were precarious and sometimes fatal. The Hungarian environment in which the Gypsies developed their art had not proven to be particularly nurturing.

For all his good intentions, Liszt was of course quite wrong about the origins of the music; as we have seen, they were unquestionably Hungarian. Ever courtly and gracious in public and private correspondence, he was surprised by the vigor of some of his critics in the ensuing journalistic battle, but nonetheless steadfastly refused to back down. The Hungarian advocates, for their part, took offense because they perceived Liszt's book as another devaluation of their culture and attempt to confiscate from them what was rightfully theirs. Hungarian political history, sadly, had for centuries made that an all-too-familiar pattern.

A second major issue for the book was authorship. Liszt's companion and lover, Princess Caroline Sayn-Wittgenstein, had had an active role in assembling the work. Liszt's students, some of whom acted as copyists, had worked from sheets in her handwriting and were under the impression that she actually wrote much of it. Caroline's daughter, Marie, defended Liszt's authorship, saying that he wrote the musical passages, that her mother wrote the nonmusical passages according to a rough sketch of his, and that Liszt's approval of these had to be secured before Caroline was allowed to let them stand.[7] In explaining this, Marie had the honesty to acknowledge her mother's influence and inclinations: "I can certainly testify how carefully Liszt weighed every word my mother wanted to smuggle in, simply because she was intoxicated by its beautiful sound."[8]

None of this was new for Liszt; his previous all-but-legal spouse (the Countess Marie D'Agoult) also had had literary aspirations and later a real writing career. It appears that some early pieces Liszt did for a Parisian music journal were not wholly his own work either; Mme. D'Agoult had helped finish certain of them.[9] In the case of *Des Bohémiens,* Liszt took full responsibility when objections to the book were raised, protecting both his own name and his coauthor's reputation, and it is really unclear if this was justice or chivalry.

There are many passages in *The Gipsy in Music* where we immediately suspect the princess's interference simply because they are far off the subject: verbose, rambling, pseudo-philosophizing pages that serve no purpose. In all fairness, however, other examples of Liszt's own writing do not seem to be appreciably different. There is general agreement that the musical passages are unquestionably his, and we saw from the quotations included in chapter 5 that these were hardly examples of clear and concise journalistic prose; rather, they were rambling, flowery, and not at all to the point. It seems to me rather too facile to blame the princess, as traditionally has been done, for stylistic excesses that Liszt himself shared.

The authorship problem reached crisis proportions with the release of the later, expanded edition. Rather than being worked out with Liszt, the expansions were largely wholesale additions from the princess.[10] The first edition had contained unpleasant comparisons between the Jews and the Gypsies, contributed by the princess and largely ignored when the book appeared;[11] in the later version these passages became far more slanderous. The Gypsies are idealized and ennobled; the Jews are presented in all ways as a contrast to that noble ideal. Suffice it to say that the princess's brand of Catholicism was of a particularly rigid variety, although the same cannot be said for Liszt's. The issue blew up in the press, the public support from the Wagnerite faction fanned the flames, Liszt protected Caroline's involvement, and things became very ugly. Despite Liszt's naïveté in the way he dealt with the issue, I do not believe one can find any evidence of antisemitism in his character. He had many Jewish friends and colleagues throughout his life and counted many Jews among his students. It is a measure of his incomprehension that he was able to write, years after all of this had occurred:

> Germans reject my music as French, the French as German, to the Austrians I write gypsy music, to the Hungarians foreign music. And the Jews loathe me, my music and myself, for no reason at all.[12]

As Alan Walker points out, still later editions of this book have Marie trying to edit out her mother's spurious additions, so that, finally, the question of authorship becomes an insoluble problem. Even apart from this issue, though, *Des Bohémiens* has other glaring idiosyncracies, lapses in style, and quirks of approach that would never be tolerated today. Even the idealized Gypsies get some shockingly paternalistic, not to say grossly insulting, treatment that is offered without apology, for examples:

> This is a people which neither associates itself with the joys or griefs, nor with the prosperity or misfortune, of any other; and which, as if it were Sarcasm itself in person, ridicules both the ambitions and the sorrows, the struggles and the festivities, of all others.[13]

> It happens that, by a strange anomaly, the Gipsies are endowed with a remarkably strong sense of self-preservation; in spite of their apparent refusal to form part of the human race.[14]

> Authority, law rule, principle, precept, obligation, duty—these are all notions and things insupportable to this strange race; not only because to admit them would necessitate an amount of reflection and mental applica-

tion which would be most repugnant to it, but also because, in the alternative case, it enjoys all the chance consequences of a life without object or result—a life the idle vagabondage of which is subject only to the incitation of imagination and desire.[15]

> Destiny has created [the Gypsy] man, but he does not know how to act as man. He cannot form and model himself according to his own will, in transporting to the domain of action the inspirations which he has either drawn from Nature or expressed in Art. They have moved and distracted, but have not *stimulated* him.[16]

> Completely and exclusively occupied with themselves, these big children do in most things precisely as little ones. They never, for instance, consider anything from the standpoint of anyone else, and still less do they seem capable of assimilating an idea. And everyone knows how disobedient and sometimes cruel children are, even in their innocent games; and that contradiction never causes them to reflect, but rather makes them more determined to obtain what they want. They are indifferent to the fate of any being or object which is not connected with their pleasures of the moment; and, in their anxiety to satisfy each desire at once, they seize what belongs to others as freely as if it were their own.[17]

It is very curious for a book purporting to discuss the musical style and defend the character of the Gypsies to depict their behavior as at best marginally human. They are likened to children, capable of neither rational action nor empathy for the rest of humanity. To the twentieth century, this sounds suspiciously like historical justifications of racism or slavery. Again, the two-author problem casts doubt on the princess. Her aristocratic background could well have allowed her to go only so far toward acceptance of the incorrigible tribe to which Liszt was so attached; for the rest, their obvious lack of propriety required an explanation, which in comparing them to children and savages is what she could have tried to provide.

Once again, however, she is too convenient a scapegoat. The book appeared under Liszt's name, and to him must go the responsibility of the perspective and the tenor of the contents, if not every last word and exaggeration. Alan Walker feels, with some reason I think, that one strong impetus for this book was in a sense religious: Liszt, with his innate virtuosity and religiosity, had an inner need to prove that art came directly from God rather than man, as it seemed to have done for him, and as it apparently did for the Gypsies.[18] His musical talent manifested itself early, without much training, and while later years saw a great deal of serious work, systematic study was never part of the picture for him. Similarly, during his lifetime most Gypsy musicians were not musically literate and seemed never to practice. Whatever their social idiosyncracies, it was clear to Liszt that a primitive (no matter how idealized) tribe with such a priori musical knowledge was living, walking proof of the Almighty's work and the necessity of art to the basic human condition.

But for the purposes of our study, this point is secondary, as are concerns about his ethnomusicological approach, authorial control, or even racial stereotypes. Liszt is a unique figure in the development of the *style hongrois* for the simple reason that, with the appearance of *Des Bohémiens,* he was the ony musician to put down on paper in specific terms what he felt the language signified. As he was one of the foremost exponents of the style, and as the book was written with a direct relationship to the *Rhapsodies hongroises* (intentionally a compendium of the Gypsies' musical style) in mind, this amounted to a frank statement of purpose. One phrase from Liszt, the performance indication to the seventh Hungarian Rhapsody, may be taken as emblematic: *"À exécuté à la façon hautaine et mélancolique des Tziganes* (To be played in the haughty and melancholy style of the Gypsies)."

II

Melancholy and haughtiness sum up the issue for Liszt. As we read in his book:

> Who could even sound the depths of that profound abyss of suffering endured by Gipsies through many generations—outcasts; all born to misfortune, degradation, hazard, and want?[19]

> It [the Gypsy race] maintains its individuality both by its constant association with Nature and by its profound indifference for all other men; with whom it only comes in contact for the purpose of procuring the means wherewith to live.[20]

> Of all the languages which it has been given to man to understand and make use of, music is the only one which the Gipsy has loved; and of all the sentiments which the Gipsy has sought to express in it *pain* and *pride* are the most remarkable.[21]

It is these emotions that Liszt most wants to project: the pain of the afflicted, the pride of the vanquished and misunderstood (both Gypsy and Hungarian parallels here), and the defiance of those who refuse to capitulate to majority patterns, even under the most extreme duress. (It is hard to avoid remembering Schubert in this context.) These emotions center on the self, as do all the characteristics Liszt ascribes to the Gypsies. His conception of them as childlike beings who experience emotion, feeling, and desire on only the most elemental level is crucial because it implies that they are then able to express themselves only in music with that same kind of vividness, immediacy, and authenticity of feeling. This is what sets them apart from musicians who study and practice in a more rigorous and regimented way: with the Gypsies musical expression is absolutely natural and necessary, and with the rest of us somehow more contrived and inauthentic.

Much of this hearkens back to Romantic and pre–Romantic

notions of noble savages and the belief that civilization represents a destructive influence that distances humanity from its idealized past. Even in the face of this idealization, some of the ways in which Liszt chooses to describe the Gypsies make them the mental and cultural equivalent of farm animals:

> It is not difficult to realise the position of the Gipsy race in the absence of all intellectual culture, and the sweet leisure of well-being peaceably enjoyed. With no history, religiously preserved and set out; no revered faith, associated with manners purified by a moral code; nor any customs, sanctioned by time and imparting solemnity to domestic changes and family events; no love of country or attachment to the soil and home; it would be impossible for a people to possess a poet, capable of delivering in heroic form, active and mobile sentiments; these being precisely those which he has denied, cast forth and banished from his soul. His condition is that he is imprisoned by the passive but invincible force of inertia; which only allows him to exist and perpetuate himself on condition of remaining inaccessible to all emotions felt by his fellow men.[22]

> His desire is for the enjoyment of his passions; entirely complete, always and every time. To calm, to moderate, to mitigate, or to make them wait; to soften, bend, combat or conquer them, are to him unknown efforts; for his travelling existence gives him an excitability which, by making change his constant pleasure, leaves him little time for the brooding of any desire. He is always aspiring; but his aspirations are as indefinite as hopes must necessarily be which have no object but sensation.[23]

Despite the supposed immutability of the Gypsy character, such descriptions do offer justification, of a kind, for their supposedly mercurial temperament. Where there is no capability of rational planning and forethought, where there is only an immediate emotional reaction to animal-level stimuli, then the full range of moods and humors can easily be imagined to flicker in and out with no connection between them: pain, pride, wild sensuality, profound tragedy, hedonism, and nameless unending grief. This is an area of direct correlation between the harmonic conventions of the *style hongrois,* as discussed in chapter 5, and the Gypsy stereotype. Sudden shifts of harmony and juxtapositions of seemingly unrelated chords can clearly symbolize shifting moods and Gypsy caprice. The musical conventions that evolved from either harmonic ignorance (following Sárosi's belief) or folklike shifts of mode could now be seen as a musical representation of the Gypsy's ever-changing mood, and variable character.

III

The gestures of the *style hongrois* were not the only musical signs Liszt used with specific meanings in mind. Paul Merrick, in his book *Revolution and Religion in the Music of Liszt,* has pointed out Liszt's association of certain keys with certain ideas, for example E major with religion, A-flat major with love, C major with the everyday world and humanity, and F-sharp major with mysticism.[24] His symbolic and oft-used "cross-motif," taken from a liturgical chant, is well known and appears in many works. These gestures appear not only in religious music, it should be stressed, but also in instrumental music like the B-minor piano sonata.

The religious impulse behind these gestures was a deep-seated one. Liszt's very real disposition to piety, even in the face of his equally real pull toward sensuality, was at least as profound as his interest in the Gypsies. It is not well known, but as a young man in a period of turmoil he had toyed with the idea of entering the Church.[25] His gravitation to the Church in later life, and his vows and assumption of the title

Abbé, were therefore the continuation of an earlier pattern. His large body of religious compositions was the product of deep religious feeling, not merely the need for functional liturgical music as had been produced by church composers centuries before.

Similarly, I would suggest that there had to be a deeper attraction to Gypsydom for Liszt to have maintained his commitment to it over the decades, as he did not to other kinds of music. Pure virtuosity and transcription, to choose two examples, are areas in which his interest dropped off markedly as his life went on. It is true that there is some indication of his early interest in Hungarian music: an account survives from a performance given in childhood in which a version of the *Rákoczy March* was played.[26] What is difficult to assess in such a case is the depth of commitment, as it is quite possible that a patriotic air might simply have been regarded as "just the thing" for a Hungarian-born child virtuoso to perform and represents no more than that. A mere attraction to the way the Gypsies' music sounded would not have sustained this type of lifelong commitment: music, book, and even his temporary adoption of a Gypsy child must be considered.

National recognition, or the hope for it, would also not have proven sufficient to fuel his philo-Gypsy activities. Hungarians did not really consider his music to be a service to the national heritage and did not universally accept him as Hungarian musical spokesman to Europe. Many considered him to be vulgarly commercial, too cosmopolitan, or too interested in the Gypsies per se to be of help to Hungary. Even certain non-Hungarian musicians were discomfited by the popular associations of the *style hongrois* and did not take Liszt's essays in it seriously; Anton Rubinstein, for example, felt that they represented posturing on the composer's part— "posing before the Gypsies."[27] The question remains: for Liszt, what significance did the Gypsies and their music have?

One problem is his early confusion, as we have already seen reflected in *Des Bohémiens,* of the Gypsies' role in the creation of Hungarian music. He had an obvious identification with the Gypsies, and he felt his Hungarian roots equally strongly, so given his early, somewhat clouded understanding of the issue the *style hongrois* could testify to both affiliations. From the 1860s forward, as he began to spend more time in Budapest, he continued to write Hungarian works, but they ceased to show any Gypsy influence. Such pieces as the *Historische ungarische Bildniss* (1870–1885), *Sunt lacrymae rerum en mode hongrois* (1872), *Fünf ungarische Volkslieder* (1873), and the late *Rhapsodies hongroises* (nos. 16–19, 1882–1886) have almost no Gypsy characteristics other than the augmented second, which was instrumental in Liszt's formulation of a new "Hungarian" musical style: sometimes highly chromatic, with the sonority of the diminished triad almost constant, sometimes almost Bartókian in declamation, but wholly unrelated to the *Rhapsodies hongroises*. The music he composed after the book came out, in other words, was far more purely "Hungarian" than the works in the *style hongrois* had been.

Peter Raabe, one of Liszt's earlier biographers, felt that in the Gypsies' music Liszt heard the voice of his own homelessness. Raabe's analysis, available to English readers in summary form in a translation of Bence Szabolcsi's *The Twilight of Ferenc Liszt,*[28] is very persuasive: Liszt, he points out, uses the Hungarian-Gypsy idiom only in specified nationalistic works; were it more a part of his musical personality it would not have been kept so discrete. This is clearly the case with Schubert, as we have seen, and it is also the case with Brahms: the *style hongrois* appeared both in specifically designated works and elsewhere, in brief passages and reminiscences, or for entire movements or variations. Raabe also suggests that Liszt did not have any greater national feelings for Hungary than he did for Germany or France. This is harder to defend, but one sees his point: Liszt was raised speaking German, after all, and from late childhood through young manhood he lived in Paris and partook of French culture. However, the "Hungarian" (as opposed to *style hongrois*) works listed above testify to genuine Hungarian sentiment on Liszt's part, at least late in his life. I suspect that earlier, his Hungarian affiliation was undifferentiated from his attraction to the Gypsies—as much in his own mind as in his music.[29]

Liszt was able to enter into the spirit of the Gypsies' music because of his innate virtuosity, according to Raabe, which was like that of an actor. This, too, is credible; Liszt is equally convincing with italianate *cantabile* and ornamentation in many of his other works. *L'italianisme* was for him a wholly assumed style, particularly considering the scornful way he sometimes wrote about the Italian aesthetic, but one could make an equally strong argument for his attraction to that as to the music of the Gypsies: his transcriptions, his travels in Italy memorialized in piano pieces, and his readings of Dante with Marie D'Agoult.

Raabe's sense was that Liszt saw in the Gypsies' music an expression of their, and consequently his, homelessness. So great was his attraction to the emotional content of their music that he tried to convince himself that it was Hungarian national music, although deep down he knew otherwise. This supposed knowledge on Liszt's part is a more problematic area in Raabe's hypothesis, as Liszt's writing an entire book in defense of something he suspected not to be true makes an unlikely scenario. Of course, it would have been completely reasonable for Liszt to have identified with the Gypsies' homelessness and for his interest in them to have spun out of this initial point of identification. Had there been an idealized romantic melding of Gypsy and Hungarian circumstances in his youthful mind, as I feel there was, it would make perfect sense for him to give voice to his Hungarian-Gypsy affiliation-interest with the *style hongrois* and to produce a book to document the entire business.[30] Moreover, this does not leave us in the unfortunate position in which Raabe finds himself, trying to postulate some knowledge in Liszt's mind that lay in direct conflict to what he espoused in *Des Bohémiens*.

For all his devotion to the Gypsies' music, however, Liszt displayed some odd blind spots. One curiosity is his editorial handling of the middle section of the Schubert *Impromptu* op. 90/2. As shown in example 48a, his version thickens the texture and makes the piece more virtuosic, but by removing Schubert's second-beat accent and left-hand chord, he disposes of the syncopation that is so much a part of the effect. The passage (which he is editorially honest enough to include as a suggestion, in smaller size, while retaining Schubert's original) then becomes more "pianistic," more difficult, but decidedly less *hongrois*. For the sake of comparison, example 48b gives the same passage from Brahms's transcription of

Example 48. Arrangements of Schubert's *Impromptu* in E-flat, D. 899, op. 90/2.

48a. Liszt edition, mm. 83–86.

48b. Brahms transcription, mm. 83–90.

this work; more (although not all) of the second beat accents remain.

Another oddity is the way in which his book deals with his forebears among the western composers who used this dialect. We already saw the inexplicable treatment of Schubert; the single work with an explicit Hungarian title was given a large dollop of unfair criticism, and no mention was made of his other *style hongrois* works, including the other two Liszt himself had edited. Beethoven comes in for similar treatment, and we have to remember that Liszt admired Beethoven enough to play his sonatas and to transcribe all nine symphonies for piano solo. The first short comment is complimentary:

> That Beethoven gave it some attention is amply proved by pages of his work, several of his thoughts, and more than one of those voluptuous flights which occur in his later works.[31]

But the fuller treatment of Beethoven and Schubert together, which immediately precedes the discussion of the *Divertissement*, is a masterpiece of condescension:

It is easy to convince oneself to what an imperfect degree "civilised" musicians have penetrated the characteristics of Bohemian art on the few occasions of their occupying themselves with it when we see such masters as Beethoven and Schubert failing to produce features essential to its form, and evidently not realising that those features constitute its very essence. Both these composers, however, and especially the first were inspired by the inexpressible suffering, as also by the audacious defiance therein expressed.

Beethoven in particular had a sort of vague intuition that certain pains, suffocations of the soul, intolerable oppressions and moral inanitions, having attained a state of delirium beyond either medical aid or remedy by natural means, could only be expressed under Bohemian forms[32]—which are as foreign to our civilisation as the sentiments themselves.

This genius, therefore, after having himself tasted the dregs of the chalice of human suffering, seemed, toward the end of his life, to have arrived at the condition of soul from which Bohemian feeling first proceeds; and thus to have more than once remembered Gipsy art in his later works. But, being done without plan, cohesion, or any developed sequence of ideas, one might almost say that is bore the appearance of his not having been properly "briefed," if it were permissible to apply such an expression to so great a man.

Schubert did not, any more than Beethoven, understand that a Bohemian art existed—that it was one by itself, having nothing in common with our art, and forming (as they say in architecture) a separate style; which simply is as *it* is because the Bohemian is as *he* is.

Beethoven and Schubert both attempted to bring, as we might say, some stray portions of Bohemian art into their own; like trying to cultivate in a strange climate stray seeds which had been borne upon the wind. As both of them lived in Vienna, they were quite well enough acquainted with Bohemian music to be struck by its originality; but neither of them recognised the individuality of Bohemian sentiment, and that Bohemian art could engender only in the Bohemian type.[33]

Of course, it is anachronistic to compare Beethoven's use of the *style hongrois* to that of the others. As a composer of his time, he used it for inflections and coloring, not the rawer form of a completely "exotic" discourse that became more common in the Romantic era. But there is a curious desire to belittle Schubert's and Beethoven's work in this area, a desire uncharacteristic of Liszt's usual generosity. He is far more complimentary elsewhere about composers and works far inferior to these to make this anything but an exceptional circumstance. The problem, I believe, is that both Liszt the man and Liszt the musician identified with the Gypsies and consequently felt proprietary about the *style hongrois*. This strong personal identification blinded him to the skill and passion with which his compositional forebears, who were neither Hungarian nor particularly interested in the Gypsies, had already used this vernacular.

Here we are reminded of his famous self-description, "half-Gypsy, half-Franciscan."[34] The seemingly God-given musical virtuosity of the Gypsy, as Walker suggested, is what Liszt also found in himself. In his years as a travelling virtuoso, he had lived a life as immediately sensual as that of the Gypsies was reputed to be, and his aura and conquests among female admirers are the stuff of legend. Perhaps more important, and less well understood, is the fact that as his life went on Liszt felt the burden of increasing disappointments. For all his sponsorship of Wagner's music there is never the feeling that he was completely happy with the many "situations" in which he found himself involved through his relationship with Wagner: Wagner's romance with and marriage to his daughter Cosima; the blow that marriage dealt to her first husband, his student Hans von Bülow; the polarity between the Music of the Future and other music; and so forth.

Neither of the two long-term romantic relationships in Liszt's own life ended successfully (meaning not necessarily marriage but at least an absence of bitter regret), and he lost his mother and the dearest two of his children in a relatively short period.[35] His compositions were never as successful as his virtuosic performances had been, political considerations in Hungary (not to mention his cosmopolitan lifestyle and an inability to speak the language) made him a marginal figure there, and the peripateticism of his youth continued, growing ever paler and less desirable, into his old age. This he called "ma vie trifurquée" (my three-pronged life), in which he spent a third of each year in Budapest, in Rome, and in Weimar. In sum, endless wandering was not all he felt he had in common with the Gypsies: he also identified with their demonic virtuosity, sensuality, profound griefs, and inner defiance. Liszt, like the stereotypical Gypsy of Romantic lore, was one who knew himself to be fundamentally different from other men, unappreciated by them, but in some sense inseparable from them.

As a result of his composition, writing, and sponsorship activities, Liszt's immersion in the music, aesthetic, and ethos of the Gypsies must at one time have been near total. Doubtless, to a certain extent he fell prey to the identification with his subject that must befall any author. Under these circumstances, even a formerly admired work by Schubert might eventually come be found essentially wanting, the remoter references by Beethoven might seem even less significant, and the ephemeral light music of his own time must have seemed nothing less than a personal affront.

Liszt as author also felt at odds with traditionally educated musicians, a group about which he had mixed feelings and to which he did not belong. In the book, they are generally treated with condescension and contempt (although occasionally with respect), because he felt sure that they would be offended by the many ways in which the Gypsy art broke established musical rules of form and harmonic argument and because he felt them incapable of perceiving its emotional depth and grasping its deeper message. (On this subject, the excerpt from chapter 5 on their supposed equation of Gypsy harmonic practice with rape and parricide is a minor masterpiece.) In reality, the "educated musician" issue seems to have been something of a straw man; uncomprehendingly pedantic objections to the *style hongrois* are nowhere to be found, despite the threat Liszt seems to have felt. Indeed, such higher-profile naysayers as Berlioz and Wagner could in no way be considered systematically trained musicians themselves. The Gypsies' multifaceted deeper message, of course, was one Liszt felt he had understood since childhood, one that he was uniquely suited to understand and express. In other words, Liszt came to feel, I believe, that because of his situational similarities to the Gypsies, he was in a unique position to understand them, and to serve as their tribune to the greater musical world. The corollary to this was that in the concert realm, despite half a century or so of *style hongrois* use before his earliest experiments, he felt the dialect to be his sole prerogative, his exclusive turf.

IV

To judge from his music and prose, Liszt was the composer who felt the greatest sense of mission about his use of the *style hongrois*. The *Rhapsodies hongroises*, after all, are the most substantial work to use this vernacular in the repertoire; as a cycle, it accomplishes everything Liszt wanted it to do—evoking Gypsy performances, touching upon all possible moods, imitating instruments, and so on. Probably he also reflected the most deeply about translating the Gypsy performances ambience to the concert platform. Because of its concerted format, his most successful single work ought to be the *Hungarian Fantasia* for piano and orchestra, an arrangement of the fourteenth Hungarian Rhapsody with the addition of the *Rákóczi Song* used as a motto (excerpts from the work are given in examples 17, 19, 23c, 27a, and 35a). With these forces, there are options unavailable to a solo pianist: the orchestra can take the role of Gypsy band, and the pianist is free to represent Gypsy violinist, cimbalom virtuoso, or *tárogató* soloist, depending on the musical passage and context. The aim is for the soloist-group dynamic to be a theatrical reality, not just an approximation created by contrasting textures and types of piano writing in the solo *Rhapsodies hongroises*.

Of course, this very theatricality sometimes arouses the greatest contempt. Pieces in the *style hongrois* are treated even today as trashy popular music, sops to an uneducated audience, merely "the sort of thing pianists like." As the most unbuttoned of utterances in this genre, the *Hungarian Fantasia* provokes the greatest condescension, as illustrated by this remark from the pianist Louis Kentner: "This brilliant (though to many musicians, vulgar) showpiece is rounded off . . . with all the usual pyrotechnics."[36] These usual pyrotechnics are, of course, an irreplaceable component of a kind of a music that Liszt took with the utmost seriousness.

Despite the relatively "authentic" deployment of performing forces, this piece has one inherent problem. In a Gypsy band, the violin soloist and conductor are united in one individual, who is able to control both the solo part and the band's support of it. In the *Hungarian Fantasia*, the lack of mutual performance experience between the soloist and orchestra, and the resultant need for a separate conductor, skews the magical Gypsy equation. A Gypsy band knows its leader's personality, caprices, and flights of fancy; the supporting players are able to anticipate and follow any rhythmic idiosyncrasies purely because of long hours of playing together. Each gesture is not rehearsed myriad times, the way concert music is prepared; rather, many pieces are rehearsed, and the band gains a sixth sense about the way in which the soloist/conductor makes music.

This freedom is unavailable to a travelling concert pianist because the orchestra cannot anticipate his or her personal traits and tastes. The conductor enables the orchestra to follow the pianist, but is able to do so effectively only if the pianist is sufficiently uncapricious to be followed and "telegraphs" his intentions clearly enough for an unfamiliar conductor to understand and accommodate. The usual result is a loss of flexibility and spontaneity, which are sacrificed to the greater good of a controlled performance.

This is in direct contradiction to the style as it was understood and evoked by Liszt, and it certainly deprives the pianist of the freedom and security the Gypsy fiddlers had. At its worst, it limits the orchestra's role to bombastic interjections in an otherwise unbroken barrage of keyboard pyrotechnics, which justifiably provokes critical responses such as Kentner's quoted above. As the majority of musicians today are neither familiar with the central European musical traditions nor have been exposed to Gypsy playing, most of us are unaware of the context of Liszt's pieces and the nature of our role in recreating the magic. The result, of course, is that the present-day image of the *Fantasia* is usually reduced to "potboiler."

There is an irony here. The single piece of Liszt's that seeks to recreate the soloist-ensemble dialogue of the traditional Gypsy band is the one most susceptible to unimaginative, four-square performance. Merely played like virtuoso showpieces, without a sense of style, it loses much of its essential character and seems even shallower than merely agile performances of non-Hungarian virtuoso concerti. All *style hongrois* concerti, such as Joseph Joachim's Hungarian Concerto in D minor (op. 11, 1860),[37] run something of the same risk. But even so, flexible, rhapsodic performances are not impossible: careful communication between soloist and performer and rehearsal beforehand can ensure a performance with a great deal of freedom. In this way, the Gypsy "magic" Liszt described and transcribed may be achieved to the greatest extent possible.

But for all the theatricality and "effectiveness" of this work and the *Rhapsodies hongroises* in general, the *style hongrois* remained, for Liszt, an intensely personal language, a language (as he explicitly said) capable of expressing griefs deeper than are available to any other musical tongue. Of his compositional output, he probably would have felt the sacred works to be most important, but he devoted an entire book to the explanation of the *Rhapsodies hongroises*, which cannot be said for any of these other works or styles. The fact is, the works in the *style hongrois* spoke from a very deep part of his soul, and must therefore hold a privileged place in his *oeuvre*. What today can, in unsympathetic hands, seem to be his trashiest compositions are really those that came out of the deepest part of him: the effortless virtuoso, the wanderer, the disappointed bearer of nameless griefs, the self-styled Gypsy. The grim irony for Liszt was that by the time he reached later life and had begun writing a different kind of Hungarian music, the *style hongrois* was indeed ubiquitous, and more and more often it was carelessly used. As a result, superficially the *Rhapsodies hongroises* did not look like either a personal statement of anything or the musical testament of a unique people; they looked like cheap effects for the lowest possible musical taste. He had long felt the *style hongrois* to be a uniquely personal mode of expression, and eventually, like his church affiliation and family circumstances, it was only one more important part of his life that had turned sour.

CHAPTER 9

Brahms

I

JOHANNES BRAHMS (1833–1897) had a lifelong affection for folk and popular musics born of long practical experience. His father had been a musician, if not a terribly elevated one, and while still a child Johannes had supplemented the family income by playing the piano, supplying popular tunes and dance music to the brothels of Hamburg, the port town in which he was born and raised. Despite these inauspicious circumstances and whatever scars this experience left on his psyche, Brahms never lost his love of music in the vernacular style, and his waltzes and folksong settings testify to his ability to elevate such idioms while sacrificing none of their unpretentious charm and beauty.

As Brahms reached musical maturity, the *style hongrois* had long been an established fact of musical life. Schubert was long dead but his works were gaining in popularity and renown, Liszt was finding his Hungarian voice, and producers of popular music were finding such exotica to continue to be a ready market. In the hands of major composers, the vivid extramusical associations of the style gave it a great power, but in the hands of *Kleinmeister* the effect dwindled as the language became ever more popularized and undistinguished.

Despite its growing connotations of ephemerality and superficiality, the natural wages of any popular music, the *style hongrois* would become one of Brahms's most beloved modes of expression, used throughout his life with greater nonchalance than either Schubert or Liszt had been able to achieve. For Brahms, it was not necessarily the language of the soul's darkest cries or of a forbidden subculture. Most of his pieces in the *style hongrois* use faster tempi, project a charming, entertaining mood, and in general have a lighter touch. This is in direct contradistinction to the recurring melancholy of Schubert's Hungarian pieces or the rhapsodic flights of Liszt's. Brahms was able to benefit from both approaches: his pieces stressed the lighter, more popular Gypsy vein, but they had the deft touch of a master composer and a true lover of the style, and thus have nothing of the pale ephemerality of so many of his contemporaries' Hungarian works.

Max Kalbeck, author of an early, magisterial biography of Brahms, emphasized the role of the failed Hungarian uprising of 1848 in Brahms's exposure to and appreciation of this style. Many refugees from that struggle passed through Hamburg on their way to points west, which according to Kalbeck, led to something of a fad for things Hungarian, including the Gypsies' music.[1] This exodus would not have been a necessary precondition for Brahms to encounter the *style hongrois;* it was already well established as a vernacular style. What this political development did bring about, however, was Brahms's meeting with Edward Reményi.

Reményi was a Hungarian violinist, originally named Hoffman, who had studied with Joachim's teacher in Vienna and who excelled in the Gypsy style. Kalbeck cites two concerts in Hamburg, in November, 1849, at which Brahms could well have heard him: one was on November 10, at which he was announced to be playing some "songs of farewell" for Hungarian officers departing for America, and a similar program was given on November 19. Among his repertoire for these concerts were "Hungarian National Melodies," played in his own arrangements, for which he had a particular gift in arrangement and performance.[2]

The young Brahms met Reményi, they got along very well, and three years later (after Reményi had toured the United States) the two went on tour. Ancedotes of their travels are common in the Brahms literature: how Brahms transposed the piano part of Beethoven's Kreutzer sonata up a half-step because he had an out-of-tune piano and Reményi refused to retune, how the two musicians visited Liszt at Weimar and Brahms fell asleep during Liszt's performance of his B minor sonata, and so on. The vernacular component of the performances was highly successful, and it was through Brahms's (probably improvised) accompaniments of Reményi's Hungarian-Gypsy excursions that the style came to be an integral part of him.[3] Eventually the differences in their personalities brought their partnership to an end, and Brahms embarked upon a much more fruitful and sympathetic friendship and partnership with another Hungarian violinist, Joseph Joachim.

For Brahms, the *style hongrois* remained a musical language largely discrete from others but nonetheless prominent in his own personal vocabulary. This ability to communicate in a variety of musical tongues bespeaks both a specific skill and a particular kind of approach to music, an approach becoming old-fashioned by the mid-nineteenth century. While Wagner cursed the public, exalted the life of the free artist, and composed dramatic works of ever-increasing size and length, Brahms (like his younger contemporary, Dvořák) composed for both the concert hall and the home. They both excelled in larger forms, such as symphonies and concerti, and in chamber music, which could serve as either concert music or *Hausmusik*. Following the older tradition of composer as craftsman, though, they both composed living-room music for unabashed amateurs, and they elevated the genre in doing so. The piano duet literature, the very essence of *Hausmusik*, would be poor indeed if it were not for the contributions of these two composers.

It is noteworthy that Dvořák's contributions to this repertoire, the *Slavonic Dances,* the *Legends,* and the suite *From the Bohemian Forest,* are among his most "characteristic" music. The duets are superbly crafted, but their musical materials are quite "popular" in style: dance melodies, folklike tunes of an eastern European cast, and an endless variety of colorful textures. Such immediately attractive music provided a composer's real financial support, not symphonies and operas, so this music had a ready market. The vast majority of composers produced tasteless ephemera in this genre; the best composers produced enduring music, even masterworks of a kind.

It is in this category of apotheosized *Hausmusik* that much of Brahms's output in the *style hongrois* belongs. There are clear uses in the more substantial chamber works as well, but for the most part his use of that language is reserved for music intended for the home. This has far less to do with the appearance of Edward Reményi in Hamburg than with a sure sense of popular taste and musical forms no doubt acquired in the blue-collar piano experience of his youth. We see it in his works based on popular waltz forms, we see it again in the folksong settings. Perhaps most clearly, we see it in the works using the *style hongrois.*

II

Brahms's most obvious uses of this vernacular are the two sets of *Ungarische Tänze* for piano four-hands, published in 1869 and 1880, which represent some of the highest-level *Hausmusik* in existence. Their popularity was both instantaneous and long-lasting; Brahms himself arranged the first ten for piano solo and then orchestrated three of these, and some were also orchestrated by his friend Dvorák.

For all of their success, most discussions of these pieces have centered around identifying the Hungarian songs on which they were based. They are played often, but are usually felt to be musically self-evident, and thus not to merit inquiry. Unfortunately for historians, Brahms's communications with his publisher Simrock about these pieces are not very enlightening. The extant letters concern details of publishing and presentation and, in keeping with the composer's general demeanor, reveal little of how he felt about the pieces.

The second set, though equal to the first in quality, has enjoyed somewhat less popularity. In correspondence with his friend Elisabeth von Herzogenberg, Brahms begrudged himself a trivial comment or two concerning these pieces, but it is her reaction to the pieces that is most illuminating. It enables us to see how a gifted, knowledgeable amateur (the intended market) would respond to such pieces when they first appeared. As they first came into print, Brahms wrote to her:

> The Rhapsodies [op. 79] and the new "Hungarians" arrived with your letter. I wonder if you will simply jeer at them and let them go? They rather amuse me. If they should amuse you likewise be sure you tell me so. You have no idea how kindly I take to that sort of thing![4]

On July 23, 1880 Elisabeth responded:

> And now the "Hungarians"! I can well believe that
> they amuse you. Delicious as the earlier ones were, I
> hardly think you hit off the indescribable and unique
> character of a Hungarian band so miraculously then as
> now. This medley of twirls and grace-notes, this jin-
> gling, whistling, gurgling clatter, is all reproduced in
> such a way that the piano ceases to be a piano, and one
> is carried right away into the midst of the fiddlers. What
> a splendid selection you borrowed from them this time,
> and how much more you give back than you take! For
> instance, it is impossible to imagine—though I may be
> mistaken—that a melody like that E minor, Number
> 20, could ever have taken on such a perfect form,
> particularly in the second part, but for you. Your touch
> was the magic which gave life and freedom to so many
> of these melodies. What impresses me most of all in
> your performance, though, is that you are able out of
> these more or less hidden elements of beauty to make
> an artistic whole, and raise it to the highest level,
> without diminishing its primitive wildness and vigour.
> What was originally just noise is refined into a beautiful
> *fortissimo,* without ever degenerating into a civilized
> *fortissimo* either. The various rhythmical combinations
> at the end, which seem to have come to you so apropos,
> would only fit just there, and are amazingly effective—
> as, for example, the delightful basses in tumultuous
> Number 15. That one would be my favorite, anyway, if
> it were not for Numbers 20, 19, 18—oh, and the short,
> sweet Number 14! If I were to try and tell you all we
> have to say about these dances, I should have to quote
> passage after passage, until I had copied out nearly the
> whole of the "Hungarians." I am longing to hear you
> play them.[5]

To her, Brahms finds "hidden elements of beauty," and
"raises" (without sanitizing) them above the "primitive wild-
ness and vigor" of the band of fiddlers. Obviously what
pleases her most is Brahms's retaining the unbuttoned vernac-

ular feel without the crudeness sometimes associated with folk-style performances.

Chamber music with strings could be played either by gifted amateurs or by professionals in concert, and Brahms left some noteworthy *style hongrois* works in this repertoire as well. The finale of the Piano Quartet in G Minor, op. 25, is one of the earliest of Brahms's many Gypsy finales, and it bears the indication *Rondo alla Zingarese*. A wild *friska,* this work has uneven phrases, spondees, and an abundance of Gypsy fire. Again, the comments of one close to the composer give a clear indication of how the work was being received. The Hungarian-born Joseph Joachim initially referred to it as "bubblingly characteristic,"[6] later commenting wryly, "You have given me a sound thrashing on my own territory."[7] This is particularly high praise since it is at this time that Joachim was composing his own op. 11, a D minor violin concerto "in the Hungarian manner," which Brahms admired, but which is far more "German" and constrained than Brahms's own Hungarian essays.

The G minor is, incidentally, the only Gypsy-finale to be explicitly designated as such. The finale of the A major piano quartet, op. 26, also uses the *style hongrois,* but its major key and prevailing elegance lend it a pronounced Viennese *Tafelmusik* feel. Brahms allowed finales such as those from op. 26, the op. 34 Piano Quintet, the Piano Concerto no. 1, and the Double Concerto to let their varying levels of Hungarian content speak for themselves, without subtitles. As the *style hongrois* became part of the everyday musical language, it grew to be associated with final movements, where tradition suggested that a lighter mood, melodic attractiveness, and rhythmic impetus might be more appropriate than the working-out of weighty artistic thoughts usually associated with sonata-allegro opening movements. As we have seen, this usage can be traced back through Schubert to Haydn.

Hungarian Dances and Gypsy-finales represent Brahms's most concentrated use of the *style hongrois*. At the other end of the spectrum would be a piece like the eighth variation from his *Variations on a Theme of Robert Schumann* for piano four-hands, op. 23. The opening of this variation is shown in example 49: the minor mode, flickering chromatics, and plaintive parallel thirds and sixths lend the piece a subtle Hungarian-Gypsy tint, but not the abandon of the G minor quartet finale. This lighter Hungarian touch is reminiscent of a work such as the slow movement of Schubert's Piano Trio op. 100, in which the minor tonality, the wan, exhausted tread, and characteristic ornaments lend a sense of Gypsy tragedy and bleakness to a work much less explicit than, say, the *Divertissement à l'Hongroise*. Brahms's use of the dialect with varying intensities is thus closer to the Schubertian tradition than to the Lisztian one.

Example 49. Brahms, *Variations on a Theme of Robert Schumann* for piano four-hands, op. 23, variation 8, opening.

Another example of Brahms's use of the *style hongrois* in the context of a variation set is seen in nos. 13 and 14 from the *Variations on a Theme by Händel,* op. 24 (the openings of each are shown in example 50). Without disturbing the flow of the set as a whole, the two form a subset, a miniature *czárdás* with doleful *lassan* and rambunctious *friska*. Variation

Example 50. Brahms, *Variations on a Theme of Händel*, op. 24.

50a. Variation 13, opening.

50b. Variation 14, opening.

13 begins in the parallel minor, with crying sixths, offbeat bass strums, and copious ornamentation. It repeats the melody in the relative major, a common device in Hungarian songs, in bar 3. By contrast, variation 14 has romping sixths, pronounced syncopations, buzzing trills, and a sudden Hungarian harmonic twist to the mediant in bar 3. While both variations evoke the *style hongrois,* they are so brief as to represent less a profoundly Hungarian statement than a simple display of compositional cleverness in casting a Baroque theme as a *czárdás.*

In the lengthy list of Brahms's works using this idiom, a couple of works are explicitly Hungarian but atypically cast: the *Variations on a Hungarian Song* for piano, op. 21/2, and the *Zigeunerlieder* for vocal quartet, op. 103 (later arranged for solo voice). The theme of op. 21/2 has prominent syncopations and alternating three- and four-beat measures, but uses negligible Gypsy material in the variations. At the other extreme, the *Zigeunerlieder,* brimming with such Hungarian characteristics as syncopations and parallel sixths, illustrates how far the *style hongrois* had come into the musical mainstream. Since Hungarian Gypsies were not known for vocal music, and since singing was never part of the traditional *style hongrois,* a vocal work such as this can fairly be interpreted as a celebration of that style, but no longer even an evocation of it.

But a work of this kind exemplifies the final stages of the *style hongrois.* Pieces for voice were atypical, particularly in the earlier stages of the style. Examples such as the numbers from Weber's *Freischütz* and the songs from Schubert's *Winterreise* stem from exceptional circumstances: the desire to encode additional meanings into a theatrical work or a song cycle. The same is true with Liszt's *Drei Zigeuner;* his peculiar proprietary approach to the *style hongrois* obviously engendered this explicitly texted minimanifesto of it. By Brahms's time, the extramusical associations of the *style hongrois* were being buried by the very ubiquity of the music in the popular sphere. Accordingly, he tended to write in the charmingly upbeat mood far more than the lamenting one, thereby accommodating the taste for the pleasant. The *Zigeunerlieder*, as charming characteristic music for the amateur market, certainly fit into this mold. The long tradition of amateur music of a Hungarian-Gypsy cast was thus outlasting the uses and approaches of the more profound exponents of the style.

In direct contrast to this trend is one of his most heartfelt uses of the *style hongrois*. It was written very late in his life, and occurs in the second movement of the Clarinet Quintet, op. 115. Brahms first sets out a sweet, lyrical D major theme at the beginning of the movement (shown in example 51). With almost Bachian didacticism, he then demonstrates, in the middle section, how the descending opening figure of the theme might inspire an improvisatory Hungarian exegesis (already shown in chapter 5, example 20). The clarinet has a rhapsodic *hallgató* solo, the strings have crying parallel sixths, and the entire mood bespeaks a wailing Gypsy lament.

Excepting occasional wispy and highly ambiguous reminiscences in the late piano works, this clarinet solo is Brahms's last statement in this dialect. It is peculiarly fitting that it is not light and dance-based, as most of his other Hungarian statements were. The *hallgató* style is one he used relatively little, so the fact that his final statement should be an introspective exploration of this kind provides a peculiar closure to his use of the Hungarian idiom. It demonstrates beyond a doubt that his command of this mood, too, was total.

In Brahms's lifetime, the context of the *style hongrois* can be seen to have undergone a gradual but profound change. For the most part, to him Hungarian-Gypsy music meant Gypsy color and popular culture, not grief, rejection, or

Example 51. Brahms, Quintet for Clarinet and Strings, op. 115, II, opening theme.

ostracism. It was now a fully accepted popular music, no longer a dialect reserved for only the most vivid and profound emotions. Elisabeth von Herzogenberg's effusive comments on the second group of *Hungarian Dances* suggest just what Brahms probably wanted to evoke: the Gypsy band in all its rude and fun-filled beauty, not the *Weltangst* associated with the circumstances of their less-fortunate fellows and perceived so vividly by Schubert and Liszt.

Brahms is really the last composer to speak this dialect as a mother tongue. It did not represent for him, as it did for Schubert and Liszt, the musical language of last resort when all else failed, but his years of performing it gave him a more intimate familiarity with it than could be had by those who merely heard it in cafés. He approached the *style hongrois* with the same skill he applied to all his musical languages: vernaculars, quasi-archaic styles, German symphonic. As Elisabeth von Herzogenberg implied (and few could disagree), Brahms may have reached the summit of *style hongrois* use: a thoroughly vernacular feel while avoiding crudity, the discovery of hidden beauties without sacrificing the feel of a scratching, shrieking Gypsy band, in short maintaining the best of both worlds, vernacular and cultivated. It is somewhat ironic that Brahms, who did not have a personal agenda with his use of this music, would bring it to its furthest development. On the other hand, as Brahms was the foremost musical linguist of the nineteenth century, anything less than absolute command of the Hungarian-Gypsy idiom might strike us as odd. His mastery proves that the language and its range of emotional expression could be mastered from purely musical experiences: hearing and performance. Ultimately, the personal affiliations with the Gypsies felt by Schubert and Liszt were not prerequisites to eloquent communication in the *style hongrois*.

CHAPTER 10

Decline and Disappearance

BY THE END of Brahms's life, the *style hongrois* was ubiquitous as entertainment music of the café type and through familiarity had lost much of its quality of strangeness. Likewise, the Gypsy stereotype, with its forbidden and alluring aspects, was an old and familiar tradition; paled by time and repetition, it became as shallow as much of the Gypsy music composed for the amateur market. In this wide and superficial use of the *style hongrois,* composers began to soften its rougher edges so as to make it less crude and unrestrained. An angular, exotic dialect that had once signified both wild freedom and insupportable grief would, obviously, not be its most effective when laboring under restraints that made it more polite and easier to digest for a broad audience. It was the beginning of the end, as the Gypsy idiom was gradually becoming a series of tired clichés rather than a vibrant musical dialect.

This twilight period saw the blossoming of a new genre, the Gypsy operetta. Johann Strauss's *Gypsy Baron* (1885),

Franz Léhar's *Gypsy Love* (1910), and the Hungarian-Vien-
nese shows of Imre [Emmerich] Kálmán (not to mention the
later American copies) featured prominent use of not only
the *style hongrois* but also the waltz. The composers of these
entertainments had the Viennese sensibility in mind, after all,
and by this advanced time Gypsy entertainers probably excelled in the waltz along with everything else. The Hungarian-Gypsy musical conventions themselves were undergoing
a leavening process, a sample of which is given in example
52. This is a piano reduction of a chorus from the first act of
Léhar's *Gypsy Love;* characteristic rhythms include *alla zoppa,*
spondees, and anapests, but these are mixed and matched in
a wholly improbable fashion that results, uncharacteristically,
in even four-bar phrasing. (Actually, omitting every fourth
bar, the offending half notes, would go a long way toward
rectifying the problem.)

Example 52. Léhar, *Gypsy Love*, opening chorus from Act II
(reduction).

Similarly, the plot reduces the complexities of the Gypsy
stereotype to pap. Ilona is the daughter of a Rumanian noble,
betrothed in a match of duty, who meets Jozsi, an alluring

Gypsy musician. Fearing the constraints of her future and desiring to escape with Jozsi, she sings,

> You are Jószi the Gypsy, and your fiddle sings of the love I am missing. . . . It calls with a magic compelling! Free must I be, free from any bond; free like you! . . . Ask me no more, but take me far away! . . . I long for freedom!

In the third act, he makes his position clear:

> I'm a Gypsy vagabond, free the wide world over; hating, loving, fierce and fond, evermore a rover! 'Tis Gypsy love you asked me for, then take it now, or leave me!

Allusions that in an earlier time might have been oblique are now baldly stated, and a character that might have inspired both dread and desire is a long way from either. Even making allowances for the offending translation, the devaluation of the entire Hungarian-Gypsy climate is clear. Nonetheless, works such as these, and imitations of them, testify by their popularity to the final "taming" of the *style hongrois*. The music remains on the less-vivid, "amateur" level of deployment, but is elevated to the largest commercial market and theatrical circumstance. The once-powerful Gypsy stereotype is sanitized and coupled with the denatured music to sing of a completely stock kind of romantic allure, a bland and largely unthreatening Other, a thoroughly prescribed kind of freedom, and to produce a wholly prescribed and inoffensive exoticism.

It would not be fair to imply that no works of any value appeared after Brahms's death. Ravel's *Tzigane* (1924) for violin and piano (later orchestrated) is a marvelous recreation of the Gypsy mood and language as filtered through Ravel's own Impressionistic sensibility. His exposure to the style was secondhand, however; a friend had played him Gypsy tunes so that he might immerse himself in the style. He certainly had no connection with it comparable to those of the earlier composers. Late works of the quality of *Tzigane* are clearly exceptional, though; it seems that in the end the very success and ubiquity of this style weakened it through over-familiarity.

The pattern is not hard to understand. Beside the continuing tradition of *Hausmusik,* in its early stages the *style hongrois* as a musical language had a very real extramusical significance, as we have seen: its link with the supposedly threatening and largely unknown Gypsies. To communicate such deep, dark, forbidden associations, a music has to be off-limits, or at least disturbing or indecipherable, to at least some segment of the musical world. As the nineteenth century progressed, the very power and expressivity of this dialect made it highly successful, and thus encouraged Gypsy musicians to proliferate, and more and more people made its acquaintance and demanded more such music. As everyone came to play it, it came to symbolize light music and to be featured in operettas, and its ability to reach the deeper emotional regions was effectively neutralized. It became an overworked collection of formulas whose former powerful and mysterious associations were now tiresome and trivial. In Hungary in 1931, Béla Bartók was under no illusions when he wrote the following:

> The music that is nowadays played "for money" by urban gypsy bands is nothing but popular art music of recent origin. The role of this popular art music is to furnish entertainment and to satisfy the musical needs of those whose artistic sensibilities are of a low order. This phenomenon is but a variant of the types of music that fulfill the same function in Western European countries; of the song hits, operetta airs, and other products of light music as performed by salon orchestras in restaurants and places of entertainment. That this Hun-

garian popular art music, incorrectly called gypsy music, has more value than the abovementioned foreign
trash is perhaps a matter of pride for us, but when it is
held up as something superior to so-called "light music," when it is represented as being something more
than music of a lower order destined to gratify undevel-
oped musical tastes, we must raise our voices in solemn
protest.[1]

As more and more musical energy moved to North America, fewer and fewer people had any firsthand knowledge of
Hungarian Gypsies anyway, and any associations deeper than
"mystery," "romance," "freedom," and "music" (plus perhaps a residual hint of baby stealing) were lost, except for
what could be reinvigorated by fiction and popular literature.
The Rom in the United States were neither numerous, relatively speaking, nor particularly disposed to music in a high-
profile sort of way, so their relation to the stereotype was
even more distant than had been the case for the European
Gypsies. Coincidentally, it was the musical and cultural
developments in the United States, and the subsequent awareness of them in Europe, that finally sealed the fate of the *style
hongrois*.

Mention was made in the Introduction to this study of the
parallel between the *style hongrois* and jazz. Both derive from
the music of poorly understood out-groups fresh from centuries of abuse and oppression. Both peoples, Rom and
African-Americans, had darker skin, a distinctive way of
speaking, and an even more distinctive way of making music
long associated with dancing and abandon. Both the *style
hongrois* and jazz also have moods that have long signified the
expression of numberless griefs, suffering so deep as to be
inaccessible to the masses: the *hallgató* style and the blues
mood (I do not mean to oversimply the various African-
American musics; I am simply speaking of jazz, itself something of an amalgam, in very general terms). Both feature

prominent syncopations, characteristic scales and melodic inflections (blue notes and slides in jazz), and distinctive but late-developing harmonic devices (two of the most obvious in jazz are the increasingly complex chordal structure and tritone substitutions). Finally, both made the slow journey from forbidden vernacular to ubiquitous popular music, provoking interest and exercising influence among concert composers and musicians (both at home and abroad) along the way. When we think of the *style hongrois* in the same context as we do jazz, we (in America, at least) understand the paradigm of its appearance and development a good deal better.

I deliberately avoided comparing the two musical languages in the course of this study so as not to dilute the treatment of my subject. This is certainly not the place for a similar treatment of jazz, which has no lack of expert advocates, scholars, students, and practitioners. More important than the mere parallel, though, is temporal proximity between the two tongues and the fact that for the wider audience they both spoke to the same need. The *style hongrois* was in decline at precisely the time that black music was emerging and waxing in this country, as the United States itself was making the transition from exotic frontier and land of opportunity to one of the centers of Western musical activity, perhaps even *the* center. It was this exploding culture and musical market, thereafter, that were in a position to define the musical language of "the people."

As the Rom's historical presence in European society was much greater than it has been here, the *style hongrois* could only be tangential to the American psyche and taste. But the music of American blacks was of far more immediate significance. This new language was soon exported, along with all the attendant extramusical associations; the European musical communities were smitten, adopting it and remaking the new music in their own image. As the *style hongrois* paled and faded almost into oblivion, jazz gave new voice to precisely the same sensibilities and needs, both in American and in Europe. Before the onslaught of jazz, emergent, vivid, and compelling, the *style hongrois* could only continue its wane as had the Turkish Style before it.

It may be that in the final years of the twentieth century the circumstances that foster "forbidden" musical vernaculars are no longer with us. Recordings disseminate all kinds of music throughout the world with a speed that works against stylistic localization, and musics can influence one another constantly. For concert music, the ongoing search for a twentieth-century identity has admitted a variety of other musics into its realm, popular and vernacular among them, and this process blurs the distinctions that give a musical vernacular its power. In any case, the ongoing realignment of musical strata might do away with designations such as "concert music" and "vernacular music" entirely. Contrariwise, the fashionable new interest in "world musics" may evolve a new musical language to express native, agricultural, or presumably earth-based emotions inaccessible to the harried, industrialized humanoid of the very late twentieth century. Such possibilities are, in any case, far beyond the scope of this inquiry.

The reference to jazz brings up another consideration relating to the *style hongrois,* one that could easily be the subject of a separate study but which ought to be at least mentioned before I conclude this one. Like all music, the *style hongrois* is most communicative when it is performed, not read off the page for purposes of analysis. There are many recordings of works in this style, but only a limited number capture the idiosyncratic flavor the style really requires. An overview of the performance practice considerations and some representative recordings that relate to this style may serve as background for a later, more systematic inquiry.

The further we get from the heyday of the *style hongrois,* the more remote its performance traditions become. This music is not played exactly as written; for many of the gestures there are conventions of rhythmic freedom, declamation, exaggerated articulations, and noisier, jangling tone that conventional notation cannot reflect. This music is not supposed to be lovely; in other words, it aspires to the condition of a real vernacular, the one it evokes.

One of the initial challenges in interpreting the *style hongrois* is simply recognizing it. Incredibly, it can go unrecognized by interpreters not attuned to differences in musical style. This often occurs in Schubert's works; only one piece bears the title *à l'Hongroise,* and performances of other Hungarian-Gypsy works often miss the point and as a result are flat, prosaic, and lacking a vital aspect of the composer's conception. (One hears, for example, polite, "serious," nonvernacular interpretations of Gershwin's concert works where the performers have missed the point in exactly the same way.) In his book on Schubert, Hans Gal describes the problem and deals with the issue of musical vernaculars in a more general way:

> I have, by the way, a suspicion that there exists something like a language barrier. This seems to be the only possible explanation for the fact that those pieces in which the music not only suggests the local background, but breaks spontaneously into the vernacular (such as the "Trout" Quintet, the last movements of the Octet, the String Quartet in A minor, the two Piano Trios and the Piano Sonata in D major) have over and over again aroused annoyance and disdainful rejection. It is also this kind of music which offers difficulties to the "foreign" performer, because he does not understand the peculiar freedom of articulation which is at

least as important for this music as the right speed, although this too is often enough misunderstood.[2]

Toward a solution to this problem, I would like to recommend a few recordings, taken from among many, that reach the heart of this performance style. Unique in its historical value and verity is Brahms's performance, on an early Edison cylinder, of part of his own Hungarian Dance no. 1. The sound quality is awful by current standards, but on repeated listenings more and more information is revealed, and one gets an increasingly vivid picture of how the composer conceived his piece and how that rhythmic conception relates to the notation, which looks rhythmically unexceptional. A very valuable discussion of this and other period recordings is contained in Will Crutchfield's article, "Brahms By Those Who Knew Him."[3]

Another recording with its roots in the previous century is the version of Liszt's third Hungarian Rhapsody by Ervin Nyiregyházi. Nyiregyházi, a Hungarian child prodigy at the turn of the century, and an obviously eccentric personality whose career was thwarted by circumstances (some of his own making), disappeared for some five decades and made some fascinating recordings in the 1970s as a very old man. His third Hungarian Rhapsody (on the Columbia two-record set *Nyiregyházi Plays Liszt,* M2 34598, from 1978) is stylistically wonderful: he interpolates rhythmically free, cadenza-like passages that include *style hongrois* gestures other than those notated by Liszt (a practice Liszt would certainly have approved, having engaged in it himself), and a rude, vivid, and brusque tone marvellously suited to the style.

An unqualified triumph is the recording of Brahms's twenty-one Hungarian Dances by Katia and Marielle Labèque (recorded in Paris, April, 1981; reissued on Phillips CD, 416 459-2). The Labèques have such a phenomenal command of the rhythmic conventions, variety of effects, mercurial changes of tempo and mood, and, above all, abandon of the *style hongrois* that the recording simply beggars description. I would happily offer this recording as a school of Hungarian-Gypsy interpretation.

One postscript: in 1988, the amusingly named Gajo Records released a record entitled *Café Noir* (GR 1001). The group itself bears the same name, and the brief, stream-of-consciousness liner notes point up both the Romani origin of at least one of the musicians and the Romani stylistic influence. Yet, while there is prominent violin and clarinet, there is also prominent guitar, played in a style not terribly remote from jazz guitar legend Django Reinhardt (himself a Gypsy). Whether Django was a Hungarian Gypsy or of some other group I cannot say, but there was no appreciable *style hongrois* in his music. The selections on this highly enjoyable album include arrangements of a Paganini Caprice (of course, the A minor theme and variations) and a work by Villa-Lobos. The cross-pollination apparent on this recording illustrates how diluted the *style hongrois* can become at this very late time, when the essence of the language is an increasingly distant memory. There are borrowings from art music, jazz, the *style hongrois,* European café music, and other popular styles, combined in an entirely attractive and stylistically "inauthentic" mix of the kind only popular musicians and those conversant with (if not dependent upon) oral traditions can produce. That is, anything the musicians had ever heard is eligible to be tossed into the stew. For this reason, *Café Noir* also demonstrates, paradoxically, in the most authentic way possible how the *style hongrois* probably originated in the first place.

A Chronology of Schubert's Works Using the Style Hongrois

Work		Date composed	Date published
Moment Musical #3, f	D. 780	?1823	Dec. 19, 1823, in the almanac *Album Musical*
Octet, F [Intro. to and final movement]	D. 803	Feb.–Mar. 1, 1824	I–III, VI, 1853, op. 166, I–VI, 1889
String Quartet, a [Final movement]	D. 804	Feb.–Mar. 1824	1824, op. 29/1
Sonata, 4-hand, C ("Grand Duo") [III]	D. 812	June 1824	1838, op. 140
Ungarische Melodie	D. 817	Sept. 2, 1824	1928

This information is based on the complete Schubert worklist appearing in *The New Grove Dictionary of Music and Musicians*. The sections appearing in brackets are those in which the *style hongrois* is utilized.

Work		Date composed	Date published
Divertissement à l'Hongroise	D. 818	autumn 1824	1826, op. 54
Symphony, #9, C ("Great") [II]	D. 944	summer 1825	1840
Sonata, D [IV]	D. 850	Aug. 1825	1826, op. 53
Impromptus, op. 90 [#2 in E-flat]	D. 899	?Sept. 1827	1827, op. 90, 1–2
Fantasy, C major, violin/piano	D. 934	Dec. 1827	1850, op. 159
Impromptus, op. 142 [#4 in f]	D. 935	Dec. 1827	1839, op. 142
Fantasy, 4-hand, f [I, III, IV]	D. 940	Jan.–April 1828	1829, op. 103
String Quintet, C	D. 956	?Sept. 1828	1853, op. 163

Notes

Notes to Introduction

1. Miriam Karpilow Whaples, *Exoticism in Dramatic Music, 1600–1800* (Ph.D. diss., Indiana University, 1958; Ann Arbor: University Microfilms International, 1981).

2. Thomas Bauman, *W. A. Mozart: Die Entführung aus dem Serail* (Cambridge: Cambridge University Press, 1987).

3. Bálint Sárosi, *Gypsy Music* [1970], trans. Fred Macnicol (Budapest: Corvina Press, 1978).

Notes to Chapter 1

1. Bálint Sárosi, *Gypsy Music* [1970], trans. Fred Macnicol (Budapest: Corvina Press, 1978), 12. They were also called "New Hungarians" after being forcibly settled. Sárosi also claims that Gypsies can be known as "Hungarians" in parts of America, but I am unaware of this additional meaning.

2. Egon Gartenberg, *Vienna: Its Musical Heritage* (University Park: Pennsylvania State University Press, 1968); Alice M. Hanson, *Musical Life in Biedermeier Vienna* (Cambridge: Cambridge University Press, 1985); Ernst Hilmar, *Franz Schubert in His Time* [1985], trans. Reinhard G. Pauly (Portland, Oreg.: Amadeus Press, 1988); and Charles Osborne, *Schubert and His Vienna* (London: Weidenfeld and Nicolson, 1985).

3. Sárosi, 37.

4. *American Heritage Dictionary*, New College Edition (Boston: Houghton Mifflin, 1976), 1126.

5. *Cigány* in Hungarian, *zingene* in Turkish, *gyphtos* in Greek. Sárosi, 38.

6. Robert Walsh, *Narrative of a Journey from Constantinople to England* (London: Frederick Westley and A. H. Davis, 1828), 357.

7. J[ohann] G[eorg] Kohl, *Austria, Vienna, Prague, Hungary, Bohemia, and the Danube* (London: Chapman and Hall, 1843), 214. Note that this implies a high level of music literacy, an attribute not traditionally associated with Gypsy musicians.

8. Sárosi, 58–59.

9. Quoted in ibid., 23.

10. Béla Bartók, "Gypsy Music or Hungarian Music?" [1931], English translation in *Musical Quarterly* 33/2 (April 1947): 240–57.

11. Sárosi, 85–119.

12. Julius Kaldy, *A History of Hungarian Music* [1902] (New York: Haskell House Publishers, 1969), 2–3.

13. Edward Brown[e], *A Brief Account of Some Travels in Hungaria, Servia, Bulgaria, Macedonia, Thessaly, Austria, Styria, Carthinia, Carniola, and Friuli* (London: Benjamin Tooke, 1673), 17–18.

14. Quoted in Sárosi, 89.

15. Ibid., 93.

16. Benjamin Suchoff, Introduction to *The Hungarian Folk-Song* by Béla Bartók [1924] (Albany: State University of New York Press, 1981), xv.

17. Sárosi, 57.

18. Ibid., 67.

19. Bence Szabolcsi, *A Concise History of Hungarian Music,* trans. Sára Karig, trans. rev. Florence Knepler (Budapest: Corvina Press, 1964), 50–51; and Sárosi, 67.

20. Sárosi, 67, 106.

21. See Miriam Karpilow Whaples, *Exoticism in Dramatic Music, 1600–1800* (Ph.D. diss., Indiana University, 1958; Ann Arbor: University Microfilms International, 1981).

Notes to Chapter 2

1. *Kuruc* is pronounced "kuruts" and means "crusader" in Hungarian.

2. Edward Brown[e], *A Brief Account of Some Travels in Hungaria, Servia, Bulgaria, Macedonia, Thessaly, Austria, Styria, Carthinia, Carniola, and Friuli* (London: Benjamin Tooke, 1673), 70.

3. *Grosses vollständiges Universal Lexicon aller Wissenschaften und Künste,* vol. 62 (Zen–Zie) (Leipzig: Johann Heinrich Bedlar, 1749), col. 528.

4. Brown[e], 82.

5. Ibid., 87.

6. Thomas M. Barker, *Double Eagle and Crescent: Vienna's Second Turkish Siege and Its Historical Setting* (Albany: State University of New York Press, 1967), 16–17.

7. The estates were parliamentary bodies that supposedly stood in the way of absolutist rule, but that in reality were controlled by the aristocracy. Ibid., 14.

8. Ibid., 19–20. The Venetian ambassador, Molin (1661), quoted in Heinrich Kretschmayer, *Die Türken vor Wien: Stimmen und Berichte aus dem Jahre 1683,* (Munich, 1938), 27.

9. Ibid., 190.

10. John Stoye, *The Siege of Vienna* (New York: Holt, Rinehart and Winston, 1964), 170.

11. William Hunter, *Travels in the Year 1792 Through France, Turkey, and Hungary, to Vienna,* 2d ed., vol. 2 (London: Printed by T. Bensley for J. White, 1798), 165.

12. Thomas Bauman, *W. A. Mozart: Die Entführung aus dem Serail* (Cambridge: Cambridge University Press, 1987), 27.

13. Ibid., 28.

14. Ibid., 32–33.

15. Miriam Karpilow Whaples, *Exoticism in Dramatic Music, 1600–1800* (Ph.D. diss., Indiana University, 1958: Ann Arbor: University Microfilms International, 1981), 73.

16. Bauman, 62–63.

17. Bence Szabolcsi, "Exoticisms in Mozart," *Music and Letters* 37/3 (July 1956): 329–330.

18. Bauman, 65.

19. Whaples, 73.

20. Christian Friedrich Daniel Schubart, *Ideen zu einer Ästhetik der Tonkunst* [1784–85; first published 1806], ed. Fritz and Margrit Kaiser (Hildesheim: Georg Olms Verlagsbuchhandlung, 1969), 332.

21. Bauman, 67.

22. Diary entry of August 20, 1802. Louis Spohr, *The Musical Journeys of Louis Spohr*, trans. and ed. Henry Pleasants (Norman: University of Oklahoma Press, 1961), 18–19.

Notes to Chapter 3

1. Quoted in Bálint Sárosi, *Gypsy Music* [1970], trans. Fred Macnicol (Budapest: Corvina Press, 1978), 112.

2. The first English publication of the Haydn finale features the aforementioned performance instruction, "In the Gipsies' style." Later editions, including the first Viennese publication, which appeared very shortly thereafter, substitute the phrase "Rondo all'Ongarese" (this is what Sárosi cites, probably from relying on Viennese editions). Were there a need for a concrete contemporary equation between the Gypsy performance style and the Hungarian musical gestures under discussion, this would obviate it.

3. Traditionally, the anapestic foot can be either long-short-short or short-short-long; the most common *style hongrois* variety is an accented short-short-long.

4. Use of the Turkish Style in minor episodes done by others, too; another instance is the fourth movement of Haydn's String Quartet in C Major, op. 33/3.

5. Bence Szabolcsi, "Exoticisms in Mozart," *Music and Letters* 37/3 (July 1956): 327–28.

6. Ibid., 326–27.

7. Julius Kaldy, *A History of Hungarian Music* [London: William Reeves, 1902] (New York: Haskell House Publishers, 1969), 17–18.

8. Kotzebue's play *King Stephen, or Hungary's First Benefactor*, was put on in Pest in 1811 to celebrate the opening of a German theater there. Beethoven's music, commissioned for this and for the *The Ruins of Athens*, which shared the program with *King Stephen*, was well received.

9. Sárosi, 70, 73.

10. The only score of this opera in the United States is a handwritten copy in the Library of Congress, Washington, D.C.

11. Miriam Karpilow Whaples, *Exoticism in Dramatic Music, 1600–1800* (Ph.D. diss., Indiana University, 1958; Ann Arbor: University Microfilms International, 1981), 171, n. 159.

12. For example, a description of the different sorts of pilgrims on contemporary pilgrimages to the Maria-Zell holds that "the

Germans are accustomed to sing in major modes, the Slavs and Hungarians in minor." (Dr. Matthias Macher, quoted in Carl Maria Brand, *Die Messen von Joseph Haydn* [Würzburg: Konrad Tritsch Verlag, 1941], 145–46).

13. Papp, Géza, "Die Quellen der 'Verbunkos-Musik': Ein Bibliographischer Versuch," *Studia Musicologica* 21 (1979): 151–217; 24 (1982): 35–97; 26 (1984): 59–132. This three-part article is a bibliography of much of this music, complete with many incipits.

14. "*Der ungerische Tanz hat einige originelle Wendungen, und die Heidemachen haben sogar Originalmelodien, die sich den Tänzen der Zigeuner ziemlich nähern. Der Tact is immer zweyviertel, die Bewegung mehr langsam als schnell, und in der Ausweichung ganz bizarr; z.B. sie beginnen vier Tacte in G, und hören so dann in C auf; und so haben sie noch manche barocke Wendungen. Dieser Tanz verdient sehr auf das Theater gebracht zu werden.*" Christian Friedrich Daniel Schubart, *Ideen zu einer Ästhetik der Tonkunst* [1784–1785, first published 1806], ed. Fritz and Margrit Kaiser (Hildesheim: Georg Olms Verlagsbuchhandlung, 1969), 352.

15. "Heidemak: Heathenish, crude person of restless character with worldly [moral] conduct, wild unruly youth, . . . The Hajdemaken were self-styled rebellious farmers, later robbers." Erhard Riemann, ed., *Preussisches Wörterbuch*, vol. 2 (Neumünster: Karl Wachholtz Verlag, 1981), 762. Note that in standard German, the word for Heyduck is simply *Heiduck*. The related meaning of *Heide*, heathen, also puts the music and its relation to the Gypsies in an unfavorable light.

16. Here I follow Leonard Ratner's terminology, which defines a topic as a "subject for a musical discourse." Topics were composed of musical figures or surface characteristics that were identified with a common and well-understood dance type or musical style (see his *Classic Music* [New York: Schirmer, 1980], 9–30).

Notes to Chapter 4

1. Quoted in François de Vaux de Foletier, *Les bohémiens en France au 19ᵉ siècle* (Paris: Éditions J. C. Lattès, 1981), 21.

2. Ludwig Achim von Arnim, *Isabella von Ägypten* [1812], vol. 2 of Arnims Werke, ed. Alfred Schier (Leipzig: Bibliographisches Institut, [1925]), 417.

3. Ibid., 77.

4. Clemens Brentano, *Werke,* vol. 1 (München: Carl Hauser Verlag, 1968), 1213–16.

5. For a full treatment of this myth see Alan Dundes, *The Wandering Jew* (Bloomington: Indiana University Press, 1986).

6. Arnim, 153.

7. Ibid., 154.

8. Ibid., 417.

9. Another story of Cervantes, "The Dogs' Colloquy," has another short passage about the Gypsies; this one is far nastier, but still dwells only on the vice of theft.

10. Miguel de Cervantes, "The Little Gipsy Girl," In *Exemplary Stories,* trans. C. A. Jones (Harmondsworth, Middlesex: Penguin Books, 1972), 9.

11. Ibid., 52.

12. Sir Walter Scott, *Guy Mannering* [1815] (New York: Funk and Wagnalls, 1900), 41.

13. Matthew Arnold, "To a Gipsy Child by the Sea-Shore," *The Poetical Works of Matthew Arnold,* ed. C. B. Tinker and H. F. Lowry (London: Oxford University Press, 1950), 41–44.

14. See Susan McClary's volume on this opera, *Georges Bizet: Carmen* (Cambridge: Cambridge University Press, 1992). Included in her discussion is a treatment of nineteenth-century exoticism in general and of Spaniards and Gypsies as representing the "Other" in the Parisian opera environment.

15. Bálint Sárosi, *Gypsy Music* [1970], trans. Fred Macnicol (Budapest: Corvina Press, 1978), 13.

16. Christian Gottfried Daniel Stein, *Nachtrage zu dem Geographisch-statistischen Zeitungs-, Post-, und Comtoir-Lexicon,* vol. 2 (N.p. 1822–24), 911.

17. *Österreichische National-Encyklopädie,* vol. 6 (Vienna, 1837), 247.

18. William Macmichael, *Journey From Moscow to Constantinople in the Years 1817, 1818* (New York: Arno Press and New York Times, 1971), 68.

19. Robert Walsh, *Narrative of a Journey from Constantinople to England* (London: Frederick Westley and A. H. Davis, 1828), 323.

20. *Bilder-Conversations-Lexikon, für das deutsche Volk* (Leipzig: F. A. Brockhaus, 1841), 801.

21. *Grosses vollständiges Universal Lexicon aller Wissenschaften und*

Künste, vol. 62 (Zen–Zie) (Leipzig: Johann Heinrich Bedler, 1749), col. 523.

22. *Bilder-Conversations-Lexikon,* 801.

23. Walsh, 324–25.

24. Ian Hancock, *The Pariah Syndrome* (Ann Arbor: Karoma Press, 1987), 58–59.

25. *Grosses Lexicon,* col. 521.

26. *Österreichische National-Encyklopädie,* 247.

27. *Bilder-Conversations-Lexikon,* 802.

28. Walsh, 327–28.

29. *Bilder-Conversations-Lexikon,* 801.

30. Ibid., 801.

31. Walsh, 325.

32. David Mayall, *Gypsy Travellers in Nineteenth-Century Society* (Cambridge: Cambridge University Press, 1988), 76.

33. Hancock, 58.

34. Ibid., 51.

35. Ibid., 58.

36. *Grosses Lexicon,* col. 526.

37. Ibid., col. 529.

38. *Österreichische National-Encyklopädie,* 247.

39. Hancock, 20.

40. *Österreichische National-Encyklopädie,* 247.

41. Walsh, 328.

42. J[ohann] G[eorg] Kohl, *Austria, Vienna, Prague, Hungary, Bohemia, and the Danube* (London: Chapman and Hall, 1843), 214.

43. Quoted in Marilyn R. Brown, *Gypsies and Other Bohemians: The Myth of the Artist in Nineteenth-Century France* (Ann Arbor: UMI Research Press, 1985), 1.

44. Ibid., 2.

Notes to Chapter 5

1. Franz Liszt, *The Gipsy in Music* [*Des Bohémiens et de leur musique en Hongrie,* 1859], trans. Edwin Evans, 1881 (1926; reprint, London: William Reeves, 1960), 307.

2. Bálint Sárosi, *Gypsy Music* [1970], trans. Fred Macnicol (Budapest: Corvina Press, 1978), 73.

3. Julius Kaldy, *A History of Hungarian Music* [London: William Reeves, 1902] (New York: Haskell House Publishers, 1969), 8, 16–17.

4. Liszt, 303.

5. Ibid., 270.

6. Ibid., 308–9.

7. Ibid., 306.

8. Ibid., 307–8.

9. Sárosi, 245.

10. Liszt, 300.

11. Sárosi, 218–19.

12. Liszt, 164.

13. Ibid., 312.

14. I refer the reader once again to the three-part article on *verbunkos* sources by Géza Papp in *Studia Musicologica;* many incipits are given, and in these the presence of this dotted rhythm is well-nigh constant.

15. James Huneker, *Franz Liszt* (New York: Charles Scribner's Sons, 1911), 162–63.

16. Sárosi, 96.

17. Let me politely disengage myself, here, from discussions of medieval theory centering on the original nature of modes as scale types, melody types, or groups of pitches sharing a final. By "traditional Lydian mode" I mean a major scale with a raised fourth degree.

18. Sárosi, 98–99.

19. This letter is cited and discussed in Paul Merrick, *Revolution and Religion in the Music of Liszt* (Cambridge: Cambridge University Press, 1987), 131–32.

20. There is an authorship problem involving this book which will be examined in more detail in chapter 8.

21. Liszt, 13.

22. Sárosi, 115.

23. Liszt, 297.

24. Ibid., 299.

25. Ibid., 301.

Notes to Chapter 6

1. John Warrack, *Carl Maria von Weber* [1968] (Cambridge: Cambridge University Press, 1976), 52–53.

2. Warrack, 240–41.

3. Pius Alexander Wolff, *Preciosa* [verse play in four acts after

Cervantes' *La Gitanilla*; prose original, 1811] (Leipzig: Philipp Verlag, [1821]), 16–17.

4. Ibid., 27–28.

5. Ibid., 41.

6. Ibid., 44.

7. This anecdote is repeated throughout the Weber literature. See, for example, Warrack, 241.

8. Carl Maria von Weber, *Sämtliche Schriften,* ed. Georg Kaiser (Berlin and Leipzig: Schuster and Loeffler, 1908), 218.

9. A frequent problem with this number is that too fast a tempo obliterates any recognizable Hungarian inflection. (Weber's indication, *Allegro feroce ma non troppo,* suggests that he foresaw precisely this danger.)

Notes to Chapter 7

1. Otto Erich Deutsch, ed., *Schubert: A Documentary Biography,* trans. Eric Blom [1946] (New York: Da Capo Press, 1977), 211–12.

2. Spaun quoted in Otto Erich Deutsch, ed., *Schubert: Memoirs by His Friends,* trans. Rosamond Ley and John Nowell (London: Adam and Charles Black, 1958), 137.

3. Quoted in Deutsch, *Documentary,* 241, 248.

4. Quoted in Deutsch, *Memoirs,* 294.

5. Quoted in Deutsch, *Documentary,* 301.

6. Ibid., 295.

7. Translation based on Philip L. Miller, *The Ring of Words* [1963] (New York: W. W. Norton, 1973), 250–51.

8. Ibid., 256–59.

9. Ibid., 258–59.

10. Bálint Sárosi, *Gypsy Music* [1970], trans. Fred Macnicol (Budapest: Corvina Press, 1978), 213–14.

11. J. A. Westrup, "The Chamber Music," in *Schubert: A Symposium,* ed. Gerald Abraham (London: Oxford University Press, 1952), 96–97.

12. Ibid., 108.

13. Schönstein, quoted in Deutsch, *Memoirs,* 103.

14. Spaun, quoted ibid., 134.

15. Anselm Hüttenbrenner, to the Schubert biographer Ferdinand Luib, Feb. 23, 1858, quoted ibid., 67.

16. Schönstein, quoted ibid., 103.

17. See Mária Domokos, "Ungarische Verbunkos-Melodie im Gitarrenquartett von Schubert-Matiegka," *Studia Musicologica* 24 (1982): 99–112.

18. Maurice J. E. Brown, *The New Grove Schubert* (New York: W. W. Norton, 1982), 37.

19. Ibid., 323. Nothing suggests that Schubert either did or did not see this work. The extent to which he admired Weber suggests that he might have made himself aware of it, particularly since the theater was well known to him. Incidentally, Helmina von Chézy, the librettist for *Rosamunde,* would write an article defending her work for the *Wiener Zeitschrift* of January 13, 1824 in which she referred to *Preciosa* as "weighty," which to the modern sensibility it certainly is not. (Quoted ibid., 322.) It does at least show that someone very close to Schubert, personally and professionally, was well aware of *Preciosa.* In any case, Schubert's use of the *style hongrois* clearly came after his intimate exposure to *Der Freischütz.*

20. Schwind, quoted in Deutsch, *Documentary,* 327.

21. Quoted in ibid., 339.

22. Maynard Solomon, "Franz Schubert and the Peacocks of Benvenuto Cellini," *19th-Century Music* 12/3 (Spring 1989): 204.

23. Quoted in Deutsch, *Documentary,* 374–75.

24. Here I follow the dating outlined in Robert Winter, "Paper Studies and the Future of Schubert Research," in *Schubert Studies: Problems of Style and Chronology,* ed. Eva Badura-Skoda and Peter Branscombe (Cambridge: Cambridge University Press, 1982).

25. Quoted in Deutsch, *Documentary,* 458.

26. Quoted in ibid., 432.

27. The wandering motif is certainly not limited to the Gypsies in Schubert's work. *Die Schöne Mullerin* and *Winterreise* speak to the same preoccupation.

28. Quoted in Deutsch, *Documentary,* 516.

29. Ibid., 528.

30. Ibid., 538.

31. Ibid., 670.

32. Ibid., 679.

33. Ibid., 681.

34. Ibid., 919.

35. Another approach to the way Schubert's sexuality may relate to his music is found in Susan McClary's "Constructions of Subjec-

tivity in Schubert's Music," found in *Queering the Pitch: Essays in Gay and Lesbian Musicology,* ed. Philip Brett, Gary Thomas, and Elizabeth Wood (New York and London: Routledge, 1993). The author was kind enough to send me her article in manuscript.

Notes to Chapter 8

1. *Bohémien* is one of the French words meaning "Gypsy." The Gypsies originally ventured into France from the east, the direction of Bohemia, hence the original misnomer, which has been preserved along with *Tzigane.*

2. Franz Liszt, *The Gipsy in Music* [*Des Bohémiens et de leur musique en Hongrie,* 1859], trans. Edwin Evans, 1881 (reprint, London: William Reeves, 1960), 363–64.

3. Quoted in Bálint Sárosi, *Gypsy Music* [1970], trans. Fred Macnicol (Budapest: Corvina Press, 1978), 143.

4. Quoted in ibid., 144.

5. Liszt, *Gipsy in Music,* 13.

6. Ibid., 275.

7. Alan Walker, *Franz Liszt: The Weimar Years* (New York: Alfred A. Knopf, 1989), 376.

8. Ibid. This information was provided by Princess Marie herself in 1911 and remained unpublished until 1932.

9. See Introduction to Franz Liszt, *An Artist's Journey: Lettres d'un bachelier de musique, 1835–1841,* trans. and annot. by Charles Suttoni (Chicago and London: University of Chicago Press, 1989), x.

10. Walker, *Weimar,* 389.

11. Ibid., 356–57, 388–89.

12. This letter is quoted on page 99 of Paul Merrick's *Revolution and Religion in the Music of Liszt* (Cambridge: Cambridge University Press, 1987), which Merrick in turn cites from Émile Haraszti in "Histoire de la Musique," in vol. 2 of the encyclopedia *La Pléiade* (Paris, 1963), 535.

13. Liszt, *Gipsy in Music,* 9.

14. Ibid., 17.

15. Ibid., 68–69.

16. Ibid., 93.

17. Ibid., 109.

18. Walker, *Weimar,* 389–90.

19. Liszt, *Gipsy in Music*, 102.

20. Ibid., 68.

21. Ibid., 107.

22. Ibid., 11.

23. Ibid., 94.

24. Merrick, 194, 195, 200, 278.

25. Alan Walker, *Franz Liszt: The Virtuoso Years* (New York: Alfred A. Knopf, 1983), 117, 132.

26. Ibid., 88–89, n. 10.

27. Quoted in James Huneker, *Franz Liszt* (New York: Charles Scribner's Sons, 1911), 156–57.

28. Bence Szabolcsi, *The Twilight of Ferenc Liszt* [1956], trans. András Deák (Budapest: Publishing House of the Hungarian Academy of Sciences, 1959), 12–13.

29. Klára Hamburger points out that he was vague on other ethnic issues involving Hungary, for example the animosity of Transylvanian Hungarians and Rumanians, or the lack of sympathy among Hungary's Saxon populace for Hungarian nationalist sentiment. See Klára Hamburger, *Liszt*, trans. Gyula Gyulás (Budapest: Corvina Press, 1980), 57.

30. In a letter of 1846 to Marie d'Agoult, he described the *Ungarische Nationalmelodien*, precursors of the *Rhapsodies hongroises*, as "half Ossianic (for there pulses in these songs the feeling of a vanished race of heroes) and half Gypsy." Quoted in Walker, *Weimar*, 380, n. 39.

31. Liszt, *Gipsy in Music*, 301.

32. This remark of Liszt's links Beethoven's use of the *style hongrois* to precisely the same associations I feel the language held for Schubert: what the composer suffered and how this language became essentially the expression of last resort for him.

33. Liszt, *Gipsy in Music*, 363–64.

34. According to Liszt, this description was bestowed on him, in German, by a Gypsy in the streets of Budapest. Letter to Carolyne Wittgenstein of August 13, 1856, from Pest. Liszt, *Correspondance*, ed. Pierre-Antoine Huré and Claude Knepper ([Paris?]: J. C. Lattès, 1987), 341.

35. Daniel died in 1859, Blandine in 1862, his mother, Anna, in 1866.

36. Louis Kentner, "The Interpretation of Liszt's Piano Music,"

in *Franz Liszt: The Man and His Music*, ed. Alan Walker (London: Barrie and Jenkins, 1970), 258.

37. This concerto provides an unwitting example for the discomfort often accorded the *style hongrois* when it is used in concert music. Donald Francis Tovey, in a highly admiring discussion and analysis of the piece, refers to the actual musical language only once, and then only to dismiss it from discussion. He makes a parenthetical reference to "the Hungarian formulas which I purposely refrain from quoting in the musical examples." The discussion appears in Tovey's *Essays in Musical Analysis*, vol. 3, Concertos [1936] (London: Oxford University Press, 1948), 106–14. As might be expected in a concerto entitled "Hungarian," the entire fabric is saturated with the *style hongrois*, and several obvious gestures are in fact included in his musical examples.

Notes to Chapter 9

1. Max Kalbeck, *Johannes Brahms*, vol. 1 (Berlin: Deutsche Brahms-Gesellschaft, 1912), 58–59; also Heinz Becker, "Johannes Brahms," in *The New Grove Late Romantic Masters* (New York and London: W. W. Norton, 1985), 79.

2. Kalbeck, 59.

3. Michael Musgrave, *The Music of Brahms* (London: Routledge and Kegan Paul, 1985), 60.

4. Johannes Brahms, *The Herzogenberg Correspondence*, ed. Max Kalbeck, trans. Hannah Bryant (New York: Da Capo Press, 1987), 105–6.

5. Ibid., 108–9.

6. Joachim, letter to Brahms of October 2, 1861. Andreas Moser, ed. *Johannes Brahms in Briefwechsel mit Joseph Joachim* (Berlin: Deutsche Brahms-Gesellschaft, 1912), 308.

7. Joachim, letter to Brahms of October 15, 1861. Ibid., 312.

Notes to Chapter 10

1. Béla Bartók, "Gypsy Music or Hungarian Music?" [1931], English translation in *Musical Quarterly* 33/2 (April 1947): 241–42.

2. Hans Gal, *Franz Schubert and the Essence of Melody* (London: Victor Gollancz, 1974), 33.

3. This article appears in *Opus* (August 1986): 14–21, 60.

Bibliography

ARTICLES

Badura-Skoda, Paul. "Possibilities and Limitations of Stylistic Criticism in the Dating of Schubert's 'Great' C Major Symphony." In *Schubert Studies: Problems of Style and Chronology*, ed. Eva Badura-Skoda and Peter Branscombe. Cambridge: Cambridge University Press, 1982.

Bartók, Béla. "Gypsy Music or Hungarian Music?" [1931]. English translation in *Musical Quarterly* 33/2 (April 1947): 240–57.

Becker, Heinz. "Johannes Brahms," In *The New Grove Late Romantic Masters*. New York and London: W. W. Norton, 1985.

Bellman, Jonathan. "Toward a Lexicon for the *Style hongrois*." *The Journal of Musicology* 9/2 (Spring 1991): 214–37.

Biba, Otto. "Schubert's Position in Viennese Musical Life." *19th-Century Music* 3/2 (November 1979): 106–13.

Cervantes, Miguel de. "The Little Gipsy Girl." In *Exemplary Stories*, trans. C. A. Jones. Harmondsworth, Middlesex: Penguin Books, 1972.

Cone, Edward T. "Schubert's Promissory Note: An Exercise in Musical Hermeneutics." In *Schubert: Critical and Analytical Studies*, ed. Walter Frisch, 13–30. Lincoln and London: University of Nebraska Press, 1986.

Crowe, David. "The Gypsies in Hungary." In *The Gypsies of Eastern Europe,* ed. David Crowe and John Kolsti. London and New York: M. E. Sharp, 1991.

Crutchfield, Will. "Brahms By Those Who Knew Him." *Opus* (August 1986): 14–21, 60.

Domokos, Mária. "Ungarische Verbunkos-Melodie im Gitarrenquartett von Schubert-Matiegka." *Studia Musicologica* 24 (1982): 99–112.

Gilbert, Arthur N. "Conceptions of Homosexuality and Sodomy in Western History." In *Historical Perspectives on Homosexuality,* ed. Salvatore J. Licata and Robert P. Petersen. New York: Haworth Press and Stein and Day, 1981. (*Journal of Homosexuality* 6/1–2 [Fall/Winter 1980–81]: 57–69.)

Hancock, Ian. "Gypsy History in Germany and Neighboring Lands: A Chronology Leading to the Holocaust and Beyond." In *The Gypsies of Eastern Europe,* ed. David Crowe and John Kolsti. London and New York: M. E. Sharp, 1991.

Harnoncourt, Nikolaus. "Comments on the performance of Mozart's *Entführung aus dem Serail.*" Program booklet to the Teldec Digital recording (1985) of *Die Entführung aus dem Serail,* conducted by the author, 29–34.

Kentner, Louis. "The Interpretation of Liszt's Piano Music." In *Franz Liszt: The Man and His Music,* ed. Alan Walker. London: Barrie and Jenkins, 1970.

Mayall, David. "Lorist, Reformist, and Romanticist: The Nineteenth-Century Response to Gypsy-travellers." *Immigrants and Minorities* 4/3 (1985): 53–67.

Papp, Géza. "Die Quellen der 'Verbunkos-Musik': Ein Bibliographischer Versuch. I: Gedruckte Werke, 1784–1823." *Studia Musicologica* 21 (1979): 151–217.

———. "Die Quellen der 'Verbunkos-Musik': Ein Bibliographischer Versuch. II: Sammlungen, 1822–1836." *Studia Musicologica* 24 (1982): 35–97.

———. "Die Quellen der 'Verbunkos-Musik': Ein Bibliographischer Versuch. III: Gedruckte Werke, 1822–1836." *Studia Musicologica* 26 (1984): 59–132.

Schünemann, Georg. "Ungarische Motive in der deutschen Musik." In *Ungarische Jahrbücher,* ed. Robert Gragger, 67–77. Vol. 4, bk. 1. Berlin and Leipzig: Walter de Gruyter, 1924.

Solomon, Maynard. "Franz Schubert and the Peacocks of Benvenuto Cellini." *19th-Century Music* 12/3 (Spring 1989): 193–206.

———. "Franz Schubert's 'My Dream.'" *American Imago* 38/2 (Summer 1981): 137–54.

Suchoff, Benjamin. Introduction to *The Hungarian Folk Song* by Béla Bartók [1924]. Albany: State University of New York Press, 1981.

Suttoni, Charles. "Liszt's Letters: A Traveling Gypsy Troupe." *Journal of the American Liszt Society* 16 (1984): 112–14.

Szabolcsi, Bence. "Exoticisms in Mozart." *Music and Letters* 37/3 (July 1956): 323–32.

Trumbauch, Randolph. "London's Sodomites: Homosexual Behavior and Western Culture in the Eighteenth Century." *Journal of Social History* 11 (1977): 15–23.

Westrup, J. A. "The Chamber Music." In *Schubert: A Symposium* [1946], ed. Gerald Abraham. London: Oxford University Press, 1952.

Winter, Robert. "Paper Studies and the Future of Schubert Research." In *Schubert Studies: Problems of Style and Chronology*, ed. Eva Badura-Skoda and Peter Branscombe. Cambridge: Cambridge University Press, 1982.

BOOKS

Abraham, Gerald, ed. *Schubert: A Symposium* [1946]. London: Oxford University Press, 1952.

Arnim, Ludwig Achim Freiherr von. *Isabella von Ägypten* [1812]. Vol. 2 of *Arnims Werke*. Ed. Alfred Schier. Leipzig: Bibliographisches Insititut, [1925].

Arnold, Matthew. *The Poetical Works of Matthew Arnold*. Ed. C. B. Tinker and H. F. Lowry. London: Oxford University Press, 1950.

Barker, Thomas M. *Double Eagle and Crescent: Vienna's Second Turkish Siege and Its Historical Setting*. Albany: State University of New York Press, 1967.

Bartók, Béla. *The Hungarian Folk-Song* [1924]. Ed. Benjamin Suchoff. Trans. M. D. Calvocoressi. Albany: State University of New York Press, 1981.

Bauman, Thomas. *W. A. Mozart: Die Entführung aus dem Serail*. Cambridge: Cambridge University Press, 1987.

Berlioz, Hector. *Memoirs of Hector Berlioz*. Annotated and edited by Ernest Newman. New York: Tudor Press, 1932.

Brahms, Johannes, *Brahms Briefwechsel* [1917]. Ed. Max Kalbeck. Tutzing: Hans Schneider, 1974.

————. *The Herzogenberg Correspondence*. Ed. Max Kalbeck. Trans. Hannah Bryant. New York: Da Capo Press, 1987.

Brentano, Clemens. *Werke*. Vol. 1. München: Carl Hauser Verlag, 1968.

Brown, Marilyn R. *Gypsies and Other Bohemians: The Myth of the Artist in Nineteenth-Century France*. Ann Arbor: UMI Research Press, 1985.

Brown, Maurice J. E. *The New Grove Schubert*. New York: W. W. Norton, 1982.

Deutsch, Otto Erich, ed. *Schubert: A Documentary Biography*. Trans. Eric Blom [1946]. New York: Da Capo Press, 1977.

————. *Schubert: Memoirs by His Friends*. Trans. Rosamond Ley and John Nowell. London: Adam and Charles Black, 1958.

Friedheim, Arthur. *Remembering Franz Liszt*. [1914–19; first published in 1961]. In *Life and Liszt*, ed. *Mark N. Grant*. New York: Limelight Editions, 1986.

Gal, Hans. *Franz Schubert and the Essence of Melody*. London: Victor Gollancz, 1974.

Gárdonyi, Zoltán. *Die ungarischen Stileigentümlichkeiten in dem musikalischen Werken Franz Liszts*. Dotoral diss. Friedrich-Wilhelms-Universität, Berlin, 1931.

Gartenberg, Egon. *Vienna: Its Musical Heritage*. University Park: Pennsylvania State University Press, 1968.

Goethe, Johann Wolfgang von. *Götz von Berlichingen* [1771]. Trans. Charles E. Passage. New York: F. Unger [1965] 1976.

Hamburger, Klára. *Liszt*. Trans. Gyula Gyulás. Budapest: Corvina Press, 1980.

Hanák, Péter, ed. *One Thousand Years: A Concise History of Hungary*. Trans. Zsuzsa Bérés. Budapest: Corvina Press, 1988.

Hancock, Ian. *The Pariah Syndrome*. Ann Arbor: Karoma Press, 1987.

Hancock, Virginia. *Brahms's Choral Compositions and His Library of Early Music*. Ann Arbor: UMI Research Press, 1983.

Hanson, Alice M. *Musical Life in Biedermeier Vienna*. Cambridge: Cambridge University Press, 1985.

Hilmar, Ernst. *Franz Schubert In His Time* [1985]. Trans. Reinhard G. Pauly. Portland, Oreg.: Amadeus Press, 1988.

Huneker, James. *Franz Liszt.* New York: Charles Scribner's Sons, 1911.

Kalbeck, Max. *Johannes Brahms.* Berlin: Deutsche Brahms-Gessell-schaft, 1912.

Kaldy, Julius. *A History of Hungarian Music* [London: William Reeves, 1902]. New York: Haskell House Publishers, 1969.

Liszt, Franz. *An Artist's Journey: Letters d'un bachelier de musique, 1835–1841.* Translated and annotated by Charles Suttoni. Chicago and London: University of Chicago Press, 1989.

———. *Correspondance.* Ed. Pierre-Antoine Huré and Claude Knepper. [Paris?]: J. C. Lattès, 1987.

———. *The Gipsy in Music [Des Bohémiens et de leur musique en Hongrie,* 1859], trans. Edwin Evans, 1881. Reprint. London: William Reeves, 1960.

———. *Letters of Franz Liszt.* Trans. Constance Bache [1894]. New York: Greenwood Press, 1969.

Lowe, Jennifer. *Cervantes: Two Novelas Ejemplares.* London: Grant and Cutler, 1971.

McClary, Susan. *Georges Bizet: Carmen.* Cambridge: Cambridge University Press, 1992.

MacDonald, Malcolm. *Brahms.* London: J. M. Dent and Sons, 1990.

Mayall, David. *Gypsy Travellers in Nineteenth-Century Society.* Cambridge: Cambridge University Press, 1988.

Merrick, Paul. *Revolution and Religion in the Music of Liszt.* Cambridge: Cambridge University Press, 1987.

Miller, Philip L. *The Ring of Words* [1963]. New York: W. W. Norton, 1973.

Moser, Andreas, ed. *Johannes Brahms in Briefwechsel mit Joseph Joachim.* Berlin: Deutsche Brahms-Gesellschaft, 1912.

Musgrave, Michael. *The Music of Brahms.* London: Routledge and Kegan Paul., 1985.

Osborne, Charles. *Schubert and His Vienna.* London: Weidenfeld and Nicolson, 1985.

Patterson, Arthur J. *The Magyars: Their Country and Its Institutions.* 2 vols. London: Smith, Elder, 1869.

Pushkin, Alexander. *Collected Narrative and Lyrical Poetry.* Trans. Walter Arndt. Ann Arbor: Ardis, 1984.

Raabe, Peter. *Franz Liszt* [1931]. Tutzing: H. Schneider, 1968.

Ratner, Leonard. *Classic Music.* New York: Schirmer, 1980.

Reed, John. *Schubert.* London: J. M. Dent and Sons, 1987.

―――. *Schubert: The Final Years.* London: Faber and Faber, 1972.

Robbins-Landon, H. C. *Haydn in England.* Vol. 3 of *Haydn: Chronicle and Works.* Bloomington: Indiana University Press, 1976.

Sárosi, Bálint. *Gypsy Music* [1970]. Trans. Fred Macnicol. Budapest: Corvina Press, 1978.

Saunders, William. *Weber.* London: J. M. Dent and Sons, 1940.

Schubart, Christian Friedrich Daniel. *Ideen zu einer Ästhetik der Tonkunst* [1784–85; first published 1806]. Ed. Fritz and Margrit Kaiser. Hildesheim: Georg Olms Verlagsbuchhandlung, 1969.

Scott, Sir Walter. *Guy Mannering* [1815]. New York: Funk and Wagnalls, 1900.

Stoye, John. *The Siege of Vienna.* New York: Holt, Rinehart and Winston, 1964.

Szabolcsi, Bence. *A Concise History of Hungarian Music.* Trans. Sára Karig. Trans. rev. Florence Knepler. Budapest: Corvina Press, 1964.

―――. *The Twilight of Ferenc Liszt* [1956]. Trans. András Deák. Budapest: Publishing House of the Hungarian Academy of Sciences, 1959.

Taylor, Ronald. *Franz Liszt, the Man and the Musician.* London: Grafton Books, 1986.

Tovey, Donald Francis. *Essays in Musical Analysis.* Vol. 3, Concertos [1936]. London: Oxford University Press, 1948.

Vaux de Foletier, François de. *Les bohémiens en France au 19ᵉ siècle.* Paris: Éditions Jean-Claude Lattès, 1981.

―――. *Le monde des Tsiganes.* Paris: Berger-Levrault, 1983.

Walker, Alan. *Franz Liszt: The Virtuoso Years.* New York: Alfred A. Knopf, 1983.

―――. *Franz Liszt: The Weimar Years.* New York: Alfred A. Knopf, 1989.

―――, ed. *Franz Liszt: The Man and His Music.* London: Barrie and Jenkins, 1970.

Warrack, John. *Carl Maria von Weber* [1968]. Cambridge: Cambridge University Press, 1976.

Watson, Derek. *Liszt.* London: J. M. Dent and Sons, 1989.

Weber, Carl Maria von. *Sämtliche Schriften.* Ed. Georg Kaiser. Berlin and Leipzig: Schuster and Loeffler, 1908.

Whaples, Miriam Karpilow. *Exoticism in Dramatic Music, 1660–1800.* Ph.D. diss., Indiana University, 1958. Ann Arbor: University Microfilms International, 1981.

Williams, Adrian. *Portrait of Liszt.* Oxford: Clarendon Press, 1990.

Wolff, Pius Alexander. *Preciosa* [verse play in four acts after Cervantes' *La Gitanilla;* prose original, 1811]. Leipzig: Verlag von Philipp [1821].

ENCYCLOPEDIAS

Bilder-Conversations-Lexikon, für das deutsche Volk: Ein Handbuch für Verbreitung gemeinnütziger Kentnisse und zur Unterhaltung, in vier Bänden. Leipzig: F. A. Brockhaus, 1841.

Grosses volständiges Universal Lexicon aller Wissenschaften und Künste. Vol. 62 (Zen–Zie), cols. 520–43. Leipzig: Johann Heinrich Bedler, 1749.

Österreichische National-Encyklopädie. Vol. 6. Vienna, 1837.

Stein, Christian Gottfried Daniel. *Nachtrage zu dem Geographisch-statistischen Zeitungs-, Post-, und Comtoir-Lexicon.* Vol. 2. N.p. 1822–24.

TRAVELOGUES

Arndt, Ernst Moritz. *Reisen durch einen Theil Deutschlands, Ungarns, Italiens, und Frankreichs in den Jahren 1798 und 1799.* Leipzig: Heinrich Graff, 1804.

Bright, Richard. *Travels From Vienna Through Lower Hungary.* Edinburgh: Archibald Constable, 1818.

Brown[e], Edward. *A Brief Account of Some Travels in Hungaria, Servia, Bulgaria, Macedonia, Thessaly, Austria, Styria, Carthinia, Carniola, and Friuli.* London: Benjamin Tooke, 1673.

Burney, Charles. *An Eighteenth-Century Musical Tour in Central Europe and the Netherlands.* Ed. Percy A. Scoles. London: Oxford University Press, 1959.

Hunter, William. *Travels in the Year 1792 Through France, Turkey, and Hungary, to Vienna.* 2d ed. 2 vols. London: Printed by T. Bensley for J. White, Fleet-Street, 1798.

Kohl, J[ohann] G[eorg]. *Austria, Vienna, Prague, Hungary, Bohemia, and the Danube.* London: Chapman and Hall, 1843.

Macmichael, William. *Journey From Moscow to Constantinople in the Years 1817, 1818.* New York: Arno Press and New York Times, 1971.

Spohr, Louis. *The Musical Journeys of Louis Spohr.* Trans. and ed. Henry Pleasants. Norman: University of Oklahoma Press, 1961.

Walsh, Robert. *Narrative of a Journey from Constantinople to England.* London: Frederick Westley and A. H. Davis, 1828.

Index